HR
IS
Sexy!

HR
IS
Sexy!

The Truth About Human Resources and
Why It's Necessary for Your Business

Delmar Johnson

HR IS SEXY!
Copyright © 2020 Delmar Johnson
All rights reserved.

Printed in the United States of America
ISBN: 978-1-64484-107-5

Delmar Johnson Enterprises, LLC; info@delmarjohnson.com; www.delmarjohnson.com

I dedicate this book to every dreamer and visionary
who decided to take a BIG risk to explore and
thrive as an entrepreneur while also making their
own impact in the marketplace,
their communities, and their families.

JOIN THE
LEAN-IN.LEARN.LEVELUP COMMUNITY

The Lean-In.Learn.LevelUp Group is a community of startups and small to midsize businesses looking to connect with and meet other like-minded dreamers who are driven, have a vision for their business and life, and want to be equipped with practical insights, strategies, and tools to make an impact in the marketplace.

Lean-In Learn LevelUp

DON'T WAIT
Join today at
www.L3Community.net

DOWNLOAD YOUR GIFTS!
FREE AUDIO LESSION & STUDY GUIDE

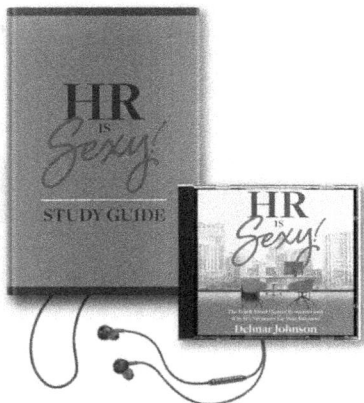

READ THIS FIRST.

Thank you for purchasing my book!
As an expression of my appreciation, I'd like to give
you the companion tools at NO COST.

DOWNLOAD YOUR GIFTS AT:
www.hrissexygifts.com

Table of Contents

Introduction

I thought for a long time about writing down my experience with and insights about this thing called human resources. To be honest with you, I wasn't sure if I
had enough useful information to create a whole book.
But one day I began thinking about all that I do know
and have shared on different platforms, from the stage,
to webinars, to audio programs, and many things in
between. All of it was done to give startups and small
businesses an inside look at how human resources plays
a part in their stage of growth, and really at every stage
of business. After spending almost half of my life, twenty-five years, in this space, I decided to take the gentle
nudging of a few smart and genuine people to write
down some things I know that could help others, and I
decided to act; so, here we are.

Twenty-five years is a long time to do anything, and
there have been many twists and turns along the way,
but one thing I can honestly say is that HR still intrigues
me—and it became even more interesting to me when I
decided to take a chance back in 2010 and act on an idea.

Allow me to give you a little background. Back in
2010 I was in a season of my life where it had flipped
completely upside down. Things had started unraveling a
few years before then, but at that point I had basically lost

everything. I won't get into the gory details of it all; however, I will say that I had been pushed to the point where I had to figure out quickly how I would regain control of my life and its surroundings. Well, after twelve years of living in other states and cities, in February 2010 I returned to my hometown, became a caregiver to an aging parent, and had to find an answer of how to acclimate back into what I had previously known.

Fortunately, I found work within a few months of returning home, and one of those jobs landed me in an HR contractor position—one that led to the conversation that sparked my brand, HR Brain for Hire™. That short but profound exchange of words went a little something like this: "Delmar, what you do here in recruiting and giving people jobs at this company seems really cool to do; I bet you could definitely do this for others that just don't know what to do." Yep, it was that quick and dirty. Sometimes it doesn't take a whole lot to spark something in you; the key is whether you decide to act on it. And often, I believe, it comes out of nowhere and catches you off guard just long enough to trigger the thoughts that could potentially open a whole new world to you. With that said, my goal was and still is to support and equip entrepreneurial leaders on the what, why, and when of human resources and how it relates to them at every stage of their business.

It all comes down to the fact that I had to find what I was good at and what I could continue to grow in, while supporting a community of individuals who had also decided to take a chance on themselves and what they believed they could accomplish, too.

Who is this book for?

This book is for entrepreneurs, startups, business coaches, authors, speakers, and small business leaders; it is for people who intentionally lead by learning the dynamics of growing a business experience beyond themselves through the establishment of processes, systems, teams, and HR infrastructure. It is for the thousands of individuals who are out there with a dream and who plan to leave a legacy through their business endeavors, and who understand that there are some not-so-glamourous steps that are a part of the process, ones that will help them get to exactly where they envision to be in their business.

What are the common problems/challenges you see with this demographic?

In supporting the entrepreneurial community since 2011, I've had the opportunity to talk and connect with hundreds, if not thousands, of businesspeople, from solopreneurs to growing, thriving small business leaders. And with every phase of business there are common problems and/or challenges. Based on past experiences, I've pinpointed the top questions that come up all the time:

1. How do you determine when it's time to hire or build a team?

2. How do you build a team when you don't have the money to hire?

3. What steps do you take when your team's performance is not acceptable?

4. How do you handle terminating somebody?

5. What kind of documentation or processes should be in your business to get things organized?

6. Where are some of the best places to attract strong employee candidates?

7. How do you overcome the fear of building a team?

This book is the solution for entrepreneur leaders

This book was written to share what I've learned over the years about a subject that many have heard of, but that not many are all that familiar with or know all the dynamics of. Let me tell you a secret: even I'm still learning, after all these years, how fluid human resources or human capital management can be. We've always gotten a bad rap; however, I have never let that stop me from serving a community of entrepreneurs who are ready to grow and expand and who have the team, money, and systems to make it all work.

How to use this book

The best way to use this book is as a guide to understanding the importance of mitigating risk through the components of human resources and how it plays a key part in the growth of your business. Read each section and then examine where you are after each defined topic to help you assess and then identify any tweaks or changes you consider necessary to strengthen your business infrastructure.

My hope is that what you find in this book will give you valuable insight, ignite great thought, and provoke you to action that is in alignment with your vision.

Delmar's innovative book is all about shaking up the HR industry. This book will teach you how to approach HR scenarios with a fresh outlook in order to get the best out of your organization's employees. The book is committed to equipping the reader with practical tools, ideas, and techniques so you can start making changes immediately. I have known Delmar since 2008 and she is committed to sharing why it is important to choose your team wisely. As the saying goes, people like to do business with those they know, like, and trust. However, without the presence of the proper company culture, the brand's image and reputation suffer. The book gives honest insight into what every business owner needs to know when building an exceptional HR Department. In this book, Delmar provides the answers you need to take your company to the next level. When you think of HR, think of Delmar Johnson.

Detra D. Davis, Founder
Foodpreneur Institute
www.foodpreneurinstitute.com

Part 1

THE TRUTH ABOUT
HUMAN RESOURCES

CHAPTER 1

Defining HR for Entrepreneurs

What is human resources?

In my twenty-five years of experience, most people I've encountered often define human resources as the "gatekeepers" of any company. I get it when people call us the gatekeepers; however, human resources is so much more than the "bad guy" in any organization.

I'll tell you a little story about how my twenty-five-year journey began. Picture this: Memphis, 1984. It was my senior year in high school, and, as with all seniors, I was embarking upon a decision about which path I would take in college and in life. My hometown always held a college event called College-a-Rama, where all the tristate area schools would convene to share information about their respective schools with all the seniors who were attending. During my visit, I talked with several representatives, and I landed on a school called MTSU and their business degree program in office management with an emphasis on human resources. I was intrigued and eventually hooked. So, when one of my senior year teachers asked me what I wanted to do when I graduated, my seventeen-year-old self said with unknowing conviction, "I'm going into human resources." At the time

11

I didn't know what human resources really was, but my understanding, and the thing that attracted me, was that it had something to do with helping people. That was the extent of my knowledge. Although that wasn't far off the mark, it didn't encompass all of what human resources is.

With all that said, allow me to formally define human resources, a.k.a. HR, a.k.a. human capital management, to set the stage for what you will read in this book. One of the most common questions is, what exactly is human resources? In layman's terms, human resources are first and foremost the people who make up the workforce within your company or business sector. They are often referred to as human capital, although that relates more to the skillset and knowledge an individual has, as well as their economic growth. Other terms you probably have heard of describing human resources are people, talent, and manpower, just to name a few. A couple more modern terms would be calling your workforce either team members or associates. And, for all of us who have been in corporate America before, we think of human resources as a division in terms of its functions, like recruiting, hiring, firing, benefits, and training.

Human resources has been through its own evolution. The precursor to today's HR used the word personnel for the functions they performed, which were described mostly as paying employees and managing the benefits they received. However, the evolution of human resources identified people as being the greatest asset and resource of a company, and now, instead of a company only paying and providing benefits to their workers, employees are hired, motivated, developed, and retained. HR is no longer like the days of old; it now has a seat at the table and is considered a strategic partner to decision makers.

Why is HR necessary for small businesses?

Many small business leaders wonder why human resources is even necessary. In my professional experience, I have often discovered that their view of human resources is a little too narrow. On many occasions when I've been asked what I do for a living and I share a little about my background, he or she always summarizes it as hiring, firing, and payroll. Trust me, it's so much more than that, as the above formal definition provided a glimpse of. Providing a little more insight into what HR does encompass helps to increase a small business owner's viewpoint, and as a result heightens their understanding in how it can and will play a part in their ability to grow and expand over time.

Why should small businesses care?

A savvy small business leader takes risks every day. It's just the cost of doing business. However, that cost can be much greater when there is no infrastructure in place, such as processes and systems to create a semblance of efficiency. Well, that describes in short why small businesses should care about human resources and all that establishes it. HR has a huge effect on the culture and environment in your workplace, setting the tone for how employees communicate with each other, settle disputes, and work with each other.

Some small businesses prefer to outsource various components of human resources, but there is no getting around it completely. Human resources management plays an integral part in how to appropriately direct people and develop a workplace culture and environment. When effectively implemented, your company's overall direction, goal, and objectives become increasingly clearer.

The elements of human resources don't just establish structure inside small businesses so that you are able to scale up; just as important is how it aids in the development of business culture. At the root of every successful business is a culture that was established from its beginning; this is why it's important to go a little deeper into what business culture looks like and how it's implemented, whether you are brand new or considered a more established business.

If you've ever wondered what it takes to transition from an entrepreneur to a small business CEO mindset, HR Is Sexy! is the book for you. I cannot tell you the initial panic I felt trying to overcome my fear around building a team and systems that will be sustainable. Delmar's passion for the success of small businesses, for them to be competitively positioned in the marketplace, is evident. From the cold hard facts of the power of human resources to the implementation of its strategies, this passion shines through and through. As an up-and-coming entrepreneur, this book provided me with practical step-by-step guidance on developing more CEO-like characteristics while implementing employer best practices that contributed to my profitable business success. This book will be a game changer for you, too!

Dr. April J. Lisbon, CEO
Running Your Race Enterprises, LLC
www.advocacycoaching.com

CHAPTER 2

Determine Your Company Culture Early

What is business culture?

Business culture, your company personality, is the starting point every entrepreneur should build as their foundation. The culture you develop as a leader becomes the driving force behind how you operate your business long-term. Many times, entrepreneurs consider culture as something that is to be established after they have a team in place or after they are making a certain amount of profits, which is not true. It doesn't matter how long you've been in business, because culture is unique to every business. Whether your business is an offline or online operation, the core values you implement and how they communicate your culture are equally important.

You may ask, what is this talk about culture all about, and why is so much importance placed on it? That's simple; ask yourself, how do you want your business to be perceived amongst your team and in the marketplace? Also consider this: in a company with no definitive cultural values demonstrated through the efficiency of their operations, the way their team is treated, or the things customers say about the level of service received, the company's reputation can and will suffer. Your reputation could potentially make or break what you're building.

When businesses shy away from investing either time or money in their culture, the consequences can be detrimental to their ability to grow. To help make the concept of culture a little clearer, let's look at five ways you can begin to incorporate or tweak a culture that will attract the kinds of customers and team that you need and will create a work environment that thrives.

1. **Be clear on your values.**

   Companies have different values that they embrace and different ways to express them; these can include:

   - **Vision:** This is a short description of what a company forecasts they will achieve or accomplish in the mid-term or long-term future. It's intended to be a compass for the actions the company will take now and in the future. **Example:** Nike's vision is "to bring inspiration and innovation to every athlete in the world." The company includes everybody in this statement; according to Nike founder Bill Bowerman, "If you have a body, you are an athlete." (panmore.com/nike-inc-vision-statement-mission-statement)

   - **Mission:** This is a short, written statement of your business goals and philosophies. It should describe your company's key functions, the markets you operate in, and your competitive advantages. A mission defines what a company is and why it exists. A mission statement has three main components—the company's mission and vision, core values that drive workplace behaviors, and key goals and objectives. **Example:** Facebook's mission is to "give people the power to build community and bring the world closer together." (www.facebook.com/pg/facebook/about)

- **Core Values:** Core values are simply the beliefs of an individual or an organization. These principles are vital in creating a work environment that your employees want to be in and where they can thrive; they help us to clearly see the difference between what's right and wrong. Core values also help a company to determine if they are headed in the right direction to meet their short-term and long-term goals and objectives. **Example:** Core values can be defined by words such as dependability, reliability, loyalty, commitment, open-mindedness, consistency, honesty, efficiency, innovativeness, and creativity.

- **Purpose**: The statement of purpose for your small business defines your company's core goals and purpose. **Example:** Whole Foods declares that "Our purpose is to nourish people and the planet."

(https://www.wholefoodsmarket.com/mission-values/core-values)

- Maybe your values include a company of integrity, innovation, creativity, strong customer service, fun atmosphere, and open communications. Great! Whichever ones you choose, just make sure you have clarity on them, so you can adequately explain them to customers and future employees.

- There are several things that could be identified as core values in your business. All of these will set the foundation you'll want to build your company on and will result in the kind of environment you want as your business evolves. Whether you have a brick and mortar or a virtual business, the core of your culture drives how you do business.

It will always start with **YOU**.

2. **Be clear on your expectations.**

   Clear expectations require you to ask yourself several questions, like:

   - What are you expecting in your business?

   - What are your goals and objectives?

   - What are some of the standards you're setting through your core values?

- What are your expectations for the people who you bring on to support you? Are you expecting that they be committed to the vision?

- Are you expecting your business to grow to a certain level over the next one, three, five, or even twenty years?

See what I mean?

Maybe you have a brick and mortar that you're looking to expand, or maybe you have a thriving online business. Either way, it's important to know what your expectations are in your own business.

3. **Be proactive in establishing processes from the beginning.**

   Take the time to be proactive and create the needed processes for your business. When you're in the beginning stage, a lot of times small business owners think, "Oh, I don't need that yet because I don't have employees." Wrong.

The key is for you to create those processes *before* you have team members, so you can begin establishing those standard operating procedures or processes to stay consistent and organized within your operations.

Maybe you started out, as most of us do, as a solopreneur. But now you've evolved into a growing small business and have your CEO hat on. Congratulations! But processes are even more imperative when you reach this stage of business, because *everyone* needs to be on the same page. It positions you to level-up as a small business CEO leader.

So, go back and think about the activities you complete each day and write them down on paper or type them up on a Word document on your computer, iPad, or whatever's most convenient for you. This exercise will help you create a visual of how your business is operating.

4. **Be clear on who your audience is and how you serve them. Understand the solution you provide your audience.**

   This is also key from the beginning. As an entrepreneur, you want to begin establishing and understanding who your audience is and how you will serve them. The clearer you are on how you address your audience's pain points, the better you know what solution to offer them for the greatest impact.

When working to understand who your target market or direct audience is and how to serve them, you must be clear about things like:

- How old is your audience?
- Where do they live geographically?
- How much do they make?
- Are they single? Married? Divorced?
- What level of education do they have?

- Where do they hang out online and offline?

If you've ever been around a business coach or strategist for more than five minutes, you've probably seen those exact questions before, or at least similar ones. The clearer you are about who you serve, the greater potential of growing a profitable and impactful business you'll have.

5. **Be clear on the direction your company is headed.**

   Do you know the direction your company is headed right now? Do you want it to grow into a Fortune 500 company or do you want to remain a small, solid, yet growing company that's serving your customers at the highest level? Not everybody, of course, is trying to be a Fortune 500 company. And that's okay. That's why we have different business models. Business is not one size fits all. You may prefer to be a solid, small business that's serving your community, or perhaps even serving from a global standpoint, with excellence. Whatever your desired end result is, get clear, concise direction on how you'll get there. It's a process, but trust me, you'll get there, wherever your *there* is, with time. **Because everything starts with you!**

Why is creating a core value-based culture important for sustainability?

If we look at business culture a little closer, I believe it will provide a clearer vision of why it directly correlates with sustainability. Intentionally creating a value-based culture—a system of ideas and perceptions about life inside an organization that basically characterizes the way people should act in the work environment—lends directly to sustainability, which is a process by which businesses manage their financial, social, and environmental risks, obligations, and opportunities. As you grow your business, the more that growth encompasses the core values you demonstrate in daily operations, the more you are in alignment with profitable sustainability in the marketplace. A values-based organization (VBO) is a living, breathing culture of shared core values among all employees. This is different from the traditional structure, which is a more machine-like, business-like approach that focuses on an authoritarian-type relationship or rigid organizational structure.

HR Is Sexy! *is the book for entrepreneurs and small business CEOs ready to build the right team with a proven methodology. With over twenty-five years of HR experience, Delmar says that "HR is so much more than just hiring, firing, and payroll" in business, and in this book she provides practical step-by-step guidance to making HR an integral part of your success in business.*

Roberto C. Candelaria
Sponsorship Strategist & Partnership Accelerator
www.RobertoCandelaria.com

PART II

PREPARING FOR LONG-TERM SUCCESS

CHAPTER 3

*Scaling Your Business Starts
with a Plan*

Strategic HR management

For anything you do in your business, having a strategy behind your next move drives how your goals and objectives will be met. It is no different when talking about being strategic in the concept of human resources management, as it applies to getting things done and in order in your everyday operations. In an effort to give some more context to an otherwise perceived heavy topic, allow me to offer some comparison.

Human resource planning in its simplest form is forecasting what your workforce will look like, and what your organizational needs will be in the future, in your efforts to achieve the goals of the business. Human resource planning is the link between the managing of human capital (people and operational functions) and the overall strategic plan. In other words, it creates a roadmap to where you are going, and there are specific and actionable elements that the planning stage has, including but not limited to:

- Recruiting and attracting qualified employee candidates

- Selecting, onboarding, and training new hires
- Following best practices in dealing with employee relations issues
- Implementing promotions or executing terminations

Strategic human resource management is the other side of the link, and its purpose is to help a company meet employee needs in the best way while promoting the goals of the company and its agenda to be competitive in the market. Human resource management should be thought of as the part of a business that will directly affect employees as referenced under human resource planning, like hiring, firing, benefits offered, salaries paid, training, and administering policies.

The importance of the strategic HR approach is that it ensures greater success for your business because you strategically developed plans for recruitment, training, and compensation based on your business goals. There is a direct correlation between the two.

Bringing strategic HR management to life

In a lesson about strategic human resource management that can be found on study.com, Katryn Stewart, who has a master's in management and teaches college courses on the subject, provides an enlightening metaphor of a basketball team on how HR management works within a company. Here's the essence of that scenario:

There is Player A that represents strategic HR, and the other players B through E are departments throughout the company. Collectively the team wants to win the ball game, and all of them may individually have outstanding skills, but no one player wins all the games. If you're a sports fan, you understand the analogy that if everybody on the team is focused on being the MVP, no one is really thinking about how to win the game by leveraging each player's strengths. It almost goes without saying that that is not how a ball game is won. A game is only won when all players are supporting each other and playing their position; the same goes with a business and how it's successfully run. In this example, Player A, the strategic side, is expected to play with the other departments, Players B through E, to meet deadlines and overall goals. Plays are defined, planned, and executed by each player; they assist when it's time to help each other complete assignments and fill in the gaps when some players are not as strong as others so as to build the strongest team. When all department players work together cohesively, the endgame is success.

An important aspect of the above analogy is that what we have known through history as "human resources" is really "people relations." This means that employees are not seen as merely assets, such as how property or inventory are considered; instead, the people within an organization are seen as a competitive advantage. The concept of people relations takes a shift in mindset and strategy, but is well worth it to create a stronger team.

Assess your next move

Assessing your business is all about gaining clarity about where your business is and where it's going. I would first like to share with you some thoughts on this. Many entrepreneurs prepare a business plan when launching a business; however, I have discovered in consulting and speaking with hundreds of them that most do not incorporate human resources planning (the how and when they will build a team) as part of their overall business strategy.

You may start out by yourself or with a few people; over time, though, it's important to properly forecast what your employment needs are going to be. Just as it is important to know potential threats to your business in the marketplace and have a plan to do something about them, failing to anticipate what your personnel needs are can have an adverse impact on your business' overall success. You want to be successful, right?

Planning for HR needs will help you to ensure that your employees have the skills and competencies your business requires to succeed. An HR plan really does work hand in hand in your overall business plan, and that helps you to determine the resources you need to achieve the business's goals. It's a good idea to prepare for the different needs of future staff that you will bring onboard via strategic recruitment and hiring, and it helps to alleviate stress when you have emergency or last-minute hiring needs. It's important to begin assessing where your business is and where you want to go. Here is a breakdown to get you started:

1. Assess your business's readiness to expand.

2. Plan out your employment needs for expansion.

3. Implement your plan, building your team one person at a time.

So, let's start with assessing your business's readiness to expand. The following is a series of questions that are integral in getting to that answer of where your business is right now and where you want to go:

1. **Are you ready to expand?** This sounds like a simple question, but it's the question to start with. The first thing to consider is whether you have a workload that justifies building a team right now. Do you have the clientele that you want, and is it really beyond you to do it by yourself? Has your client list grown to the point where you know you need to delegate some things out, whether to other professionals like yourself, to vendors, or to other types of support? Remember, building a team can include many things beyond just hiring an employee. Lastly, are the things that you have on your plate so overwhelming that you wind up doing nothing? Or, do you wind up being very slow

in providing the level of customer service that you want to give to your current client base, let alone also being able to extend yourself to gain other clients?

2.   **Are you ready to give up control?** Now this is a question that is really important to understand, because a lot of times, when you are a solopreneur or startup and you're starting out, you have this vision of what you want to happen, but you don't necessarily want to give up control and actually delegate out those things that act as distractions and are a waste of your time and talent. You want to be able to say yes to giving up some control so you can delegate those things that do not necessarily waste your time, but do really stretch you when it comes to having enough time in the day to get things done. Are you ready to give up control? That's a big question that you want to honestly ask and answer for yourself.

3.   **Can you take on more risk?** This is a big question, too. Can you take on more risk—because any time you bring someone into your business beyond yourself is a risk, right? Any time you delegate things out to someone else, you're taking a risk. You're taking a risk that they're going to do it like you want it to be done and that they will do a great job. You're taking on a risk when

you're bringing someone into the fold of your business and they learn things about it, maybe some proprietary things, maybe some confidential things, and you want to make sure that they're not going to be communicating those things to others beyond what is necessary. Ask yourself that question: can you take on more risk?

4. **What do you really need help doing?** A lot of times we get bogged down in grinding, going after new clients, trying to keep the clients that we do have, doing all the work, wearing the hats of the accountant, the bookkeeper, the owner, the facilitator, all the many hats that you wear as an entrepreneur. But have you stopped long enough to write down what it is that you really need help doing?

Doing that is not only going to give you more time to do the parts of your job that only you can do, such as going after new clients, it will also give you the power to delegate and give you the power to be able to communicate to the people who you bring on as part of your team; you will be able to hand off to them things like coordinating social media management, managing email marketing, doing research, booking you for speaking gigs, and much more. There are several things that another person can come into your business and onto your team to support. But it's imperative that you are very clear about what those things are.

5. **And then the ultimate question, can you afford it?** A lot of times when you start out, you may think you cannot afford help—but yes, you can. You can afford help even from the beginning if you have honestly answered these questions. If you've nailed down the answers to these questions and really given thought to it, then, when you approach the affordability aspect of it, the question becomes: **can you afford not to?** Can you afford not to get help when you're trying to grow your business? Because you cannot grow beyond yourself without help; that's simply a *fact*.

Ask and answer these questions for yourself to really assess your readiness to expand, now or in the future.

The other part of assessing your business is understanding what your hiring options are when you're ready to build a support team. Maybe you're working on a tight budget, or maybe you don't have a budget at all; either way, you need to consider your options when you're assessing where your business is, where you want to go, and what options will move you into the space where you want to be. I always say that the first line of defense for a startup entrepreneur is interns. There are several different types of interns, such as on-site, virtual, and eight-hour interns. We will go more in-depth about having interns, hiring contractors, and hiring employees in subsequent chapters; right now we're talking about assessing your business.

Your options are many, including interns, as mentioned above. Part-time workers are another possibility; you can build a budget around a part-time worker and be able to control your business a little bit more. Independent contractors, or freelancers as they're sometimes called, allow you to hire people on a project basis, instead of an ongoing basis; you can really budget around that, as you can fold in the cost of the independent contractors into what you've charged your clients for the projects that you have going on. If you're a nonprofit entrepreneur, volunteers are the way to go. In addition, you can source out work to other small businesses that have the expertise that you're looking for.

Create a job avatar

When it comes to truly understanding the roles you currently have or are planning to incorporate in your business, creating a job avatar, a.k.a. a job profile, will be key in guiding you to the right job candidates. The simple way to create your own job profile from scratch is to identify what positions you want to hire in your business over time, then research the specifics of what that job would include, its responsibilities, and the skill-set required to perform the job.

Here's a breakdown of what a job description could look like:

JOB DESCRIPTION TEMPLATE

Organization Name: [   ]

Title of Job: [   ]

Date: [   ]

Prepared by: [   ]

Supervisor: [   ]

MAIN RESPONSIBILITIES (WHY THIS JOB EXISTS)

Describe in one or two sentences what this position is expected to accomplish for the company.

DUTIES

List the work duties of this position in order of importance. Use action words to describe the task and include descriptions of how the tasks are to be done, if this is important.

PHYSICAL DEMANDS

Describe any working conditions that may affect some individuals' ability to do the work. Some examples might be lifting, shift work, sight requirements, etc.

SKILLS

Take it from an owner of multiple businesses: getting the HR portion of your business running smoothly is crucial if you want to have a profitable, sustaining business. If you are like me, and HR is not your strong point and you need help with even the fundamentals of getting started, then HR is Sexy! is the book for you! It takes you through the process of transitioning from an entrepreneur to a small business CEO mindset and helps you overcome the fear around building a team and systems that will be sustainable for your business. Delmar's passion for the success of small businesses to be competitively positioned in the marketplace is evident and shines through as she gives the hard, cold facts of the power of human resources when you implement its strategies and use it to your advantage. You will have practical step-by-step guidance on how you too can develop more CEO-like characteristics while implementing employer best practices that contribute to your profitable business success. Let's face it, we all want our businesses to be profitable, and we all concentrate on bringing in revenue, but not all of us understand how important it is for our HR processes to be in place to help nurture our revenue-generating efforts that push our business to the next level. If you are ready to make sure your business's foundation is strong and ready to scale, then I strongly recommend HR is Sexy! as a must-read for any entrepreneur.

Veronique Link, Founder
The Link Institute for Social & Economic Change, LLC
www.thelinkinstitute.com

Chapter 4

Achieving Your Business Goals with HR

How do the HR puzzle pieces fit your business goals?

In a business, there are plenty of moving parts to make it work every day, from operations, to marketing, to client relations, to IT support, and so forth. The key to the interdependency of each department lies with how well their human resources puzzle pieces—like recruitment and hiring or performance management—have been implemented as a basis for their capability to expand long-term. Let's explore some of those puzzle pieces that help to create the foundation for business.

Recruiting and hiring

Every business, no matter the size, needs to concern itself with recruiting and hiring, whether to fill a vacancy, staff a new position, or plan for succession for future management.

Economic conditions, business expansions, and competitive activity all affect hiring decisions. In developing a business case for recruitment, it's important for you as a growing business to consider the primary purpose of the position, the financial and operational reasons for creating or refilling an open position, and whether the duties of the job could be absorbed within any of your existing staff. If a position is not created or refilled, you as an employer may experience financial losses as a result.

The fundamentals of recruiting and hiring usually include some combination of internal and external recruitment tactics. Both approaches have certain basics in common: a foundation in job analysis, well-written job descriptions, and compliance with applicable laws, especially equal employment opportunity laws.

Performance management

When your business is growing and you've taken the leap to expand with an employee-based team, tracking performances becomes important to determine future roles and promotions and whether it's time to change the makeup of your team. Evaluating and implementing performance measurements will create a roadmap that will play a role in how employee changes will occur.

In the past, performance evaluations were all about sitting down with an employee once per year and reviewing how well they did their jobs and met predetermined objectives and goals for the year. In a 2017 SHRM.org article, reference was made of a performance management study by Mercer, an HR consultancy, that stated 89 percent of employers linked their employee pay to how well they performed during a certain evaluation period, and 57 percent used a traditional 5-point grading scale. Today, evaluations are still important; however, they are most effective when they are conducted more often throughout the year and when communication between you and your team is more transparent. This allows you to stay aware of how your employees perform, and allows you to receive critical information, keep organizational goals in mind, and empower employee teams to play a part in setting performance priorities that will lead to achieving larger, strategic objectives.

Employee development and training

A business is only as strong as its team. The right team, with the right strategy, plans, and execution, makes for business sustainability. It's important not to worry that any individual person on your team might take advantage of professional development opportunities you offer, then turn around and take their skills developed while working for you somewhere else. That's a risk you must be willing to take as a CEO leader, because being in business is risky; as your team increases their capacity and skills, there's a greater chance of them leaving if another great job comes along. However, a business culture that intentionally advocates professional development can increase employee loyalty exponentially.

Safety and wellness

The Occupational Safety and Health Administration (OSHA) has issued many new standards over the past few years, and employers need to think about how to revamp safety policies to comply with them. The key to conveying the new safety policies in the workplace is through communication, training, and accountability. If you have a brick and mortar business with employees, this is a strategy that will be very important. And there is nothing more impactful to drive home the importance of developing safety and wellness measures than through facts and statistics. Steps for reporting injury must be implemented, because documentation helps you stay compliant in your business. Safety should be at the top of the list as an important workplace concern for all employee-based organizations. The human cost of accidents is of paramount concern in the workplace. Every ten seconds an American worker is injured or becomes ill on the job. The economic cost of workplace accidents is also high—over $100 billion annually. The law requires you to provide a safe workplace—and that is beneficial to everyone.

Compensation and benefits

Statistically, compensation and benefits are the two largest overhead expenses in business, no matter the size of the business. These are the parts of human resources that are highly regulated and driven by compliance with employment laws. Both together are considered "total compensation" when it comes to hiring, and they are typically discussed during the negotiation part of an interview. Compensation is based on the defined job, demographics, and marketplace value to establish fair wages, whether the employees are hourly or exempt. Benefits take on many forms and potentially come with a very high price tag. But there are several health options available in the marketplace for both small and large companies. It is very important that you shop the market for the best and most cost-effective plan your business is positioned to financially cover.

Cross-cultural communication

We live in an increasingly global world and workplace, and communications channels can have cross-cultural dynamics when doing business. Professionals face many challenges, including dealing with cross-cultural sensitivities, as a result. As professionals, it's important to manage these kinds of challenges quickly to reduce any adverse effects on meeting targets and to keep your business running as usual. To keep up with a twenty-first century team, certain skills will be key, such as the ability to communicate, collaborate, and have awareness of cross-cultural differences within the workplace. At the end of the day, how we adjust, learn, and effectively work with a diverse culture affects productivity.

To put this in context of the importance of cross-cultural communications, there are a few familiar analogies we can look at, such as:

- **Fish in a bowl:** This analogy refers to how a fish swims in the water because it's a natural habitat, and is not aware of the nature of that water; as people, depending on the kinds of opportunities we encounter, we may or may not be conscious of our surroundings.

- **Onion:** This analogy is in reference to all of us, because we all have layers as a result of varying life experiences through work, education, and upbringing that must be pulled back and learned over time.

- **Sunglasses:** Culture enables us to frame issues. This analogy is referencing how we all look at the world through our own colored lenses. In business, however, it's important for professionals to look through the lenses of an organization or business, as leaders do.

- **Iceberg:** It is widely known that the largest part of an iceberg can't be seen because it's underwater. This correlates with all the things that can be happening with any interaction, because there is usually a lot going on underneath the surface; therefore, an effort must be made to look both above and below the surface.

We are defined by our attitudes, traditions, beliefs, and values. When those values are shared by a social group, it forms our culture. This social group ranges in size from our family or our colleagues to even as large as a nation. Culture basically drives everything we do, how we think or respond. It's something we learn and is influenced by others and the things all around us.

Starting a business is one thing. Growing and scaling is another. The latter can't be done without a solid team surrounding you and HR policies, procedures, and systems to support it. This is why HR is Sexy! is so important. And coming from Delmar Johnson, a highly seasoned dynamo who knows her stuff inside and out, this book should be every entrepreneur's go-to HR bible. Literally, keep it on your desk, because you'll be referencing it often! I've personally worked with Delmar as a client and highly recommend her expertise and know-how. Truly, HR is Sexy! is a gem you really can't go without.

Gwen Jimmere, CEO
Naturalicious
www.naturalicious.net

PART III

HIRE THE RIGHT PEOPLE

CHAPTER 5

Identifying the Best Choice

Know your options

Understanding your options when it's time to delegate helps you to better define the work and the person who is best suited to complete the assignment. Delegation is key to getting more things done through others. As a small business enterprise, so many things can get overlooked, which makes delegating one of the most essential actions you can take in fulfilling your responsibilities as a leader. Here are some specific points to keep in mind when it comes to delegation:

1. **Delegating helps you fulfill your responsibilities and improve your business.** Although we are keenly aware that we all have the same twenty-four hours in a day, seven days a week, there never seems to be enough time. But when you learn the power of delegation and how to assign work to the right people on your team, then you discover that you have more time to address key priorities. That's why it's also important to know the strengths and talents you have on your team, whether it's one person, five

people, or a hundred people. It's important to understand what their individual strengths are and what skills need more development.

2. **Delegating helps to motivate your team.** It shows the confidence that you have in your team, their abilities, and the problem-solving skills that they're able to demonstrate on the things that you delegate to them, and encourages them to develop or expand the skillset that they have right now. That's going to help you as a business owner.

3. **Delegating helps your team look beyond their own jobs or responsibilities.** When you're delegating certain things to them as they're learning, they're being empowered to look beyond what their initial job was or what their responsibilities are. Furthermore, you're adding responsibilities that will develop their skills and teach them what they need to know to move to a higher position, which will eventually be a win-win situation for the both of you.

4. **Select and explain delegated tasks carefully.** When you delegate, don't assign without explaining what the expectations and timeframes are to complete any task. Ensure they understand the elements of the task; when you communicate expectations clearly, it helps them to take ownership of it. Once you've delegated,

don't hover and micromanage. The goal is to empower them. They have the skills and abilities and you trusted them with the things that you delegated to them. That trust plays an integral part in what you're doing. Allow them to do their job and ask questions as needed for any further clarification. It's better to have clarification during the process to ensure the end result is met on time and on budget.

Once goals have been met, follow up with a complete review of the results of their assignment, the employee's performance, and how well they did with the tasks that were delegated to them. As you continue to delegate certain things out to your team, you become more efficient and strategic in covering all areas of daily operations.

Interns

As an entrepreneur, one of the many goals I'm sure you have is to grow your business, and it's hard to do that without a team of support. How to build a team from scratch is probably the number one question I'm asked by current and prospective clients. There is a sense of fear in not knowing all the dynamics of building a team through the recruitment and hiring process that usually drives that questioning. It has been my experience that approaching the "team building" process begins with the most budget-conscious way of doing it—and that's through interns.

Before I dive into building your own intern program, it's important to define exactly what an internship is. An internship is a system of on-the-job training. Interns are normally college age students, both undergraduates and graduates, although high school students can be considered as well. Student internships provide opportunities for students to gain experience in their field, determine if they have an interest in a career, create a network of contacts, or gain school credit. Interns and internships are an awesome way to begin building your team, particularly when your budget is tight or there's no budget at all.

When starting with interns, here are some guidelines you should consider first:

1. How long do you want the internship to last?

2. Will it be a one-time experience, or will it be continuous?

3. What status will the intern have, part-time or full-time, paid or unpaid? How will they be classified?

4. Will it be part of an educational program? Will they get credit for doing what they will be doing with you as an intern in your employment?

5. What tasks will the intern be assigned? Understand that an intern is not to be treated as a gofer or as a regular employee.

After this list of things to consider, you next want to be sure that this is the right time to get help. Then, it's important that you know exactly what it is you need to take off your long list of things to do for your business operations. Before you can outsource anything, it's important to know what you need and how an intern can fill that void. An important part of that is how to relinquish some control. As entrepreneurs and small business owners, a lot of times you've worked in your business by yourself for a long time, and you've worn all the hats, from marketing to accounting and everything in between. There are so many things that you do as an entrepreneur who hasn't built a team yet, and it could easily lead to a state of feeling overwhelmed.

Some of the things that an intern can help you with could include managing emails, managing your social media platforms, following up on phone calls to hot prospects and current clients, and doing research. Maybe you're needing to research a product or service that you want to offer. Another example is event planning. If you're planning a workshop, a mastermind, or a conference, these are the kind of things that a hospitality intern, for instance, can help you to plan. Or you might need assistance with project coordination. What project are you putting together that you're pulling your hair out over and could use some help with? An upperclassman intern can help you with that as well.

To go a little further into the discussion of internships, we must look at the legalities of internships. There are seven criteria for determining intern status. Other legal issues impacting internships can include international students, intellectual property, benefits and insurance, and equal opportunity employment. Let's first begin with the seven criteria "test" that's identified to determine internship status.

The test for unpaid interns and students

Before hiring any unpaid interns, there is a test to determine if an unpaid intern is appropriate for your business. It's generally called a "primary beneficiary test" as defined by the Courts, and is used by the FLSA (Fair Labor Standards Act) in determining if your intern should be termed as an employee or not. It is a method to examine the economic impact of the relationship formed between the intern and employer, and which one is the primary benefactor. The Department of Labor (DOL) provides a list of factors for consideration in your decision making. To be aware of what those factors advised by the DOL are, here's a summary of their importance:

1. Both the intern and employer are clear that there is no expectation nor promise of compensation

2. The training provided during the internship cycle should be comparable to a learning environment, including what they have learned in the classroom

3. The internship is in alignment with what is being learned in the classroom and could allow

the student to earn credits toward their academic plan

4. The internship should occur during the academic calendar year

5. The internship schedule is limited to the period in which the intern benefits

6. The intern's work should complement, not replace, that of employees currently on staff, while still being an educational experience

7. The intern and the employer understand that the intern is not entitled to a paid job once the internship is closed out

These seven criteria should always be used as a guideline and rule of thumb as you establish your own internship program. Additionally, due diligence in researching the laws of the state in which you hire interns is important, as there are many states that require interns to be paid at least the federal minimum wage rate.

International students

One legal issue to address involves international students. International students as interns can bring a new perspective to your organization. They can bring new insight from their own cultures and typically are eager to experience the professional world that's known here in the United States. The office for international programs at the student's campus will be able to advise the student regarding his or her work authorization status, particularly the type of student visa that they will have.

Intellectual property

The next legal issue that could potentially come up is with intellectual property. In some cases, interns may work on projects where intellectual property rights are a concern for your organization, so you should keep that in mind. Think of it this way: if you had an employee with access to the same information who you would ask to sign a nondisclosure agreement, you may ask an intern to do the same thing. If you are concerned about certain information getting into the wrong hands, you are encouraged to seek additional legal advice.

Benefits and insurance

A third potential legal issue impacting internships is benefits and insurance. Most college students are going to be on insurance from their school or still be under their parents' insurance.

Equal opportunity employment

Lastly is equal opportunity employment. Federal and state regulations regarding equal opportunity employment apply to the employment of interns as well as full-time employees. For further information, I would encourage you to speak to legal counsel to get the full ramifications of what that means.

It's important to have a general awareness of the legalities of internships and keep them in the forefront of your mind as you go forward in gaining interns and building your team from that perspective.

Employer benefits of interns

The benefits to employers of having interns are plenty and the list can be long, including the following:

- You gain a flexible, cost-effective workforce not requiring a long-term commitment. It's not a long-term commitment when it's about an internship. You have reduced recruitment costs while having access to a skilled labor pool.

- There's an increase in your company's productivity levels. Now everything doesn't fall on you to get things done. You have someone working with you that can work on important projects or assignments and check them off your list. Other revenue-generating activities are also an option to be given to an intern to learn and execute.

- You gain more time to pursue and capture more clients. That really is one of your ultimate goals. As an entrepreneur or small business owner, you want to have the time to pursue and capture more clients, to not necessarily just work *in* your business, but to work *on* your business as well.

- You have an opportunity to be a mentor and give back to the community; it raises the standard of professionalism of the future workplace. As the intern is learning and gleaning from you, from your skills and experience, that increases their skillsets, their experience, their knowledge level, and their talent, and they can take that out into the workplace as they begin to pursue jobs in their career.

It really is a tremendous benefit to you as an employer to have interns.

Benefits for the interns

It's not just you as the employer who reaps the benefits; there are even more benefits for the intern:

- First, the intern can test and apply classroom theory in a work environment. They have an opportunity to get clearer on their career goals as they work out what direction they want to take; the more they learn under your employment, the better they're equipped to really have clarity about the direction that they want to go.

- Another benefit for an intern is that they develop skills and increase knowledge in a specific field. They may be studying a body of knowledge in the classroom, but being able to be hands-on and really develop those skills on the job is essential. Furthermore, it's an opportunity for them to work, contribute, and learn from professionals such as yourself. That really is the key and the goal for an intern: to learn.

- Yet another benefit for an intern is to obtain marketable work experience. They're more marketable as a result of their internship experience when they graduate and are able to pursue their career path in whatever field they received their degree.

- Lastly, they make valuable business connections and contacts. That also is an advantage. It allows them to be in contact with other professionals and business owners that they can potentially contact in the future for things that they may be working on in their own life, both personally and professionally.

Identifying organizational goals

The next step in the consideration for developing an internship is identifying organizational goals and project needs. That's something that you want to have in place as you begin pursuing interns. You need a list of organizational goals so you and your interns can be on the same page.

Before you bring in an intern, create a list of potential responsibilities and projects. List possible learning exercises that the intern will be able to do when they're onboard with you. Also, identify your intern options. I'm going to be moving further into discussing what those are.

Design your intern program

You can determine the kind of intern you want by answering a couple of questions. First, will the things you want the intern to do particularly benefit them? Second, how long do you want the internship to last and when will it start?

Even in answering those questions you must look at the various types of interns, of which there are a few options to choose from.

- You have the traditional onsite intern, whether full time or part time. If you have a brick and mortar business as opposed to a virtual one, it's likely your intern is going to be onsite.

- Another type of intern you could have is an eight-hour intern. The eight-hour internship is not so commonly known; however, it is a more progressive trend in the hiring practices that are happening today. Basically, an eight-hour intern simply refers to a format where interns work only eight hours a week, whether that's onsite or offsite. Technology's so advanced now that you can have an offsite intern and still get quality work out of them. An eight-hour internship really does have several advantages to it. One is that you have higher energy interns, as students who are not overwhelmed with a full load of classes and a full-time job are simply going to be more productive. Another advantage is that there's a larger applicant pool when you're offering an eight-hour opportunity. That opens your pool of potential interns by accommodating those students who work a second job, do not necessarily live nearby, or want to come in during off hours to avoid commuters. There are several types of advantages that you find with an eight-hour intern; again, it's not the most commonly known, but it is a progressive trend that's happening now.

- You have the virtual intern. Technology has equipped us to be able to have a virtual intern; they can do their work remotely, and you can talk with the intern via teleconference call or even Skype if you want to have more of a face-to-face interchange with them.

- Then you have the combination intern. That's a combination of an onsite and a virtual intern, where they may come into your office, if you're in a brick and mortar, a couple of days a week, and the other days of the week they're virtual. You can stay in contact with them through virtual access, through Zoom or other video, or through teleconferencing platforms.

Find the right interns for your business

There are three areas I want to concentrate on when it comes to finding interns. The first one is to build relationships with your local college's career services offices. They will be your ally and can operate as the liaison between you and the interns. Because they have their finger on the pulse of the campus and know which students are looking for internships, they're one of the first places that you want to begin to build a relationship.

The second one is to tap into your own circle of professional and other business contacts. Your business contacts may have already used some great interns, and while they may have transitioned to using contractors or employees, they can refer you to potential previous interns that worked out if they think you would benefit from having those interns.

A third is to strategically use social media platforms. Although LinkedIn is still statistically considered one of the number one places to find potential help, interns typically are going to be college student age and are probably found more on Twitter and Snapchat. In addition, websites like www.internships.com have a large database of interns seeking an internship. Such websites are specific social platforms that, when used strategically, will yield qualified prospective interns and graduate students at a higher rate.

Aspects of recruiting and hiring interns

This may be a challenging area for you in the beginning, but I have every confidence that you're going to handle it just fine.

Recruiting and hiring interns starts with a written job description. This is where expectations and duties are defined so that the intern is very clear about what it is that you want them to do. After a job description is written, you begin to post your intern job ads. Your job ads can be derived and created from your job description. There are various intern-related sites that you can post to, as mentioned previously, and for the most part it's going to be free; in addition, you can post directly to area colleges from which you are seeking interns.

Once you've posted the job ad, you will then start accepting resumes from the intern sites you've posted to. What I suggest is to designate an email address, for example a Gmail account, to receive those resumes so your business or work email address won't be inundated with resumes.

From there, begin to sort the resumes into a "keep" and a "not a match" stack. After you've categorized them, you'll begin to set up prescreen interviews from those resumes that you've chosen. As a rule of thumb, I suggest identifying the top ten for prescreening interviews. From the top ten, you're going to narrow them down and schedule direct one-on-one interviews with maybe the top three to five out of those potential prescreened resumes. Once you've gone through the direct interviews, you will make your final decision on your number one choice, or maybe, if you're looking for more than one intern, the top two.

Upon the completion of your recruiting process and making your final choice, it's then time to get things ready to bring them onboard. This includes preparing the proper paperwork to create a personnel file for efficiency in tracking the intern's general information, as well as any measures you have established to monitor their project workload and performance.

Onboarding action steps for interns

First, after your new intern has accepted your offer, you want to call and officially welcome them. Then you want to provide them with a way to contact you in the event of a question or an issue. You may want that contact to be directly with you, or you may want to have an assistant already established in your business that any questions or concerns can be channeled through.

Another onboarding action step is to create an onboarding schedule outlining the phases of getting your intern acclimated. In corporate America we just call this the orientation process; however, taking the intern through an onboarding process is a much better option. Maybe your process will last an initial week and then you progress from there, or maybe it's for only a few days; whatever your time frame, the goal should be to set them up for success.

If there's going to be a computer provided for them, make sure to set up a login and a password so they'll be able to access whatever accounts that you're going to give them access to. If there's office supplies that they're going to need, such as a legal pad, pen, paper, stapler, or whatever else may be applicable, make sure you've provided them for the intern. You may even want to order some business cards or networking cards, because if they're ever out representing you and your company, that gives them a professional look to the person who they'll be networking with or talking to. That is optional, but that's just a suggestion that I wanted to make sure that I added to the potential onboarding intern action steps for you.

What might the first day activities for new interns look like? If you have a brick and mortar, it may be important for you to distribute an assigned key and/or access card to the office if you're in a professional executive building. Another first day activity may be to review their work schedule and pay schedule, because they need to know when they're going to be working and, just as important, when they're going to be paid.

Discuss procedures for scheduling time off and unexpected absences, because even with interns, life can happen. They need to know that there are procedures in place in case of emergencies or in case something suddenly comes up.

Another first day activity could be to review appropriate attire for the workplace if you have a physical office. But even if you don't have a physical office, you may still want to tell them what the appropriate attire is, even as a virtual intern, because if they're ever going to be out representing you at an event or at a venue, then you still want them to be dressed properly.

Go over any phone information that they need. Show them where to find the fax machine, copier, and any replacement office supplies they might need. Provide computer orientation at the desk. Explain if there's a computer sign on, if there's shared drives on the network that they're going to have access to, what their email access is, and if there's a Meeting Maker or a calendar schedule that they need to know about. Make sure they understand the company's website and what kind of information they can glean from there.

You can give a tour, if you're in a physical place, showing where they can hang their coat, where the washroom is, the water fountain, the vending machine, and where the break room is. Show them the refrigerator, the emergency exit, their parking space, and all the general things that you would do for a regular employee.

Then arrange a welcome lunch for the new intern so they can really feel welcome in the space that they're going to be in, whether that's for a few weeks or a few months. You want to welcome them in and make them feel comfortable enough to experience a successful internship. These are all some of the first day activities that you might do as you begin to bring on interns.

What your new intern's first week could potentially look like

- Review job responsibilities, competencies, and expectations. That's going to be a critical conversation that you need to have right off the bat for them to be set up for success.

- Review the performance feedback and appraisal process. The intern should know how you're going to be judging them, how you're going to review their performance, and what kind of process is going to be in place in order to give them that feedback.

- Review the company's mission, strategy, values, policies, and procedures, along with the organization of the department and any critical members of your group. Go over the department calendar if you have one, and review confidentiality of information if necessary. Explain if there are any emergency regulations and, if they apply right away, give any necessary health and safety training. There may be some things that are applicable right away and some that come later.

- Review any additional training you would like them to go through. If there is a cost associated with that training, you should cover it, as there may be some training that you will want to pay for to really expand that intern's experience with you.

- Schedule weekly or biweekly meetings to touch base with your new intern so they can get feedback from you as an ongoing process, and not just for one day that may be thirty or sixty days out. Keep an eye on them and keep touching base with them, letting them know how they're doing and understanding where they are in whatever project or assignment they're working on.

It's important to go through this kind of onboarding process in the first week to set them up for success.

How to close out the internship

Closing out an internship includes evaluating the intern's performance and conducting an exit interview. Let's first look at evaluating their performance. That can be a formal evaluation or an informal evaluation.

A formal evaluation can include a few things. You can have the intern complete a competency evaluation form, or you can conduct a one-on-one intern evaluation meeting, where you're having a one-on-one dialogue to get feedback from them and provide them with good feedback about how their performance was. Go over what challenges they faced and review opportunities to improve in areas that may have been a little bit more challenging for them.

A third area of formal evaluation is to make sure they've filled any academic evaluation requirements. Generally, there's an academic advisor who is the liaison between the students and their schools and the internship program who checks to ensure the employer is offering a legit opportunity. Each academic institution is different, but often it is the responsibility of the intern to present to the employer, which is you, the necessary steps to fulfill the academic credit requirements and fill out the necessary forms for that institution. If they want to have academic requirements and you're doing an academic evaluation, they must first have the necessary paperwork and be able to relay to you upfront that that is what they're really wanting to get out of the internship.

Under an informal evaluation, you can have an informal weekly check-in. While interns can ask questions in between those check-ins, you as the supervising manager or business owner should urge them to keep a list of any non-urgent issues that don't directly affect project progress but there may still be questions that they need to have answered. This way, interns can address these on a weekly basis and don't have to necessarily hold onto them until maybe two, three, or four weeks out. That's one way to conduct an informal evaluation, just continuing to touch base with them and in the end closing it out.

In some rare cases you may need to dismiss an intern. Dismissal of an intern should only occur in severe cases, such as theft or assault, or if they brought or used drugs on the premises, especially if you're in a brick and mortar. Now, keep in mind the interns may be more immature than your employees—if you have employees right now—and may have an adjustment period while familiarizing themselves with the new working environment. That's where a learning curve may come in; but you will only want to dismiss an intern because of those severe cases of theft, assault, or drug usage. In all other cases, you want to be as understanding as possible, help guide them through the process, and be available to answer any questions that they may have. Also, utilize the evaluations as a tool to provide feedback on their performance and progress. Constructive criticism can often improve a less-than-ideal internship experience. It's very important to have that.

In conducting an exit interview, you want to give the intern an opportunity to give you feedback about what their experience was like and how they felt that you dealt with the internship. You want to be able to get feedback, even as the employer, so that if there were some challenging areas or any opportunities for improvement in your program, you can do that before you hire your next set of interns. In the exit interview you also want to potentially be able to provide a strong reference or recommendation for that intern, because if they did do an overall good job for you, that reference can be one of the things that they can walk away with as compensation, even if it wasn't a paid internship.

In closing the intern program, when you follow each of these steps, I'm convinced you will be off to a great start in reducing the feeling of being overwhelmed and replace it with a sense of accomplishment as a business owner. Building your team through the establishment of an internship program is the first step to becoming an employer of choice as you grow and increase in revenue.

Independent contractors

Eventually, as you take on bigger contracts, bigger projects, and more clients, your business will start expanding. This is an exciting time, and a potential indicator that you are transitioning from interns to needing another level of professional help. Contractors are a great way to make that transition.

It is critical that you, as a business owner, correctly determine whether the individuals that you bring on, that are providing a service for you, are employees or independent contractors. Since there is such a very thin line between contractors and employees, it's important to define what an independent contractor is and how to determine their status.

What is a contractor? The general rule is that an individual is an independent contractor if the payer, that's you as the client, has the right to control or direct only the result of the work, and not what will be done or how it will be done. That's key to remember. Generally, if you have an employee, you're paying social security taxes, Medicare taxes, and unemployment taxes on the wages that you're paying that employee, which is a distinctive factor between an employee and a contractor. With a contractor, you do not generally have to withhold or pay any kind of taxes on payments.

I've told you what a contractor is by definition, so let's dig a little bit deeper and talk about the three basic common law rules that will help you determine whether the person providing service is an employee or an independent contractor. Any information that provides evidence of the degree of control and independence of the employee must be considered when you move into this realm of your business and start wanting to hire contractors.

The three basic common law rules, as officially identified by the Internal Revenue Service, are behavioral, financial, and type of relationship. Let's dig into each one of them a little further.

Behavioral controls

The first of the common laws is behavioral controls, and that's broken down into four categories itself: 1) types of instructions given, 2) degree of instruction, 3) evaluation systems, and 4) training.

The first category is the kind of instructions given. An individual classified as an employee is generally subject to being given explicit instructions about their job by their employer, including details on when, where, why, and how the work should be performed. The following examples of such instructions are provided by the IRS as guidelines:

- When you work and where the work is performed

- What tools are to be used to get the job done

- What kinds of workers to hire or have assist to perform the work required

- Where to acquire types of supplies and services

- What specific work must be done by a designated individual

- What steps to follow when performing a job

These types of instructions are geared more toward someone who would be classified as an employee versus a contractor.

The second category of the behavioral function is the measure of how much instruction is given. This is in reference to how detailed the employer is in providing instructions and the level of control an employer would have over a worker in doing the tasks and responsibilities of the job. The greater the details, the more it's an indication the worker is and should be categorized as an employee. Less detailed instructions reflect less control, so that is an indication that the worker is more likely an independent contractor.

The third category of the behavioral function is the type of system used for measuring performance. When a performance evaluation process is measuring the details of how the work is performed, this becomes a factor that identifies a person who is categorized correctly as an employee. On the other hand, if that same performance evaluation system measures only the end results or the deliverables, it could point to being categorized as either one, an independent contractor or an employee. An employee who falls under an evaluation system that measures just the end result will generally be an individual or an employee who has a certain level of autonomy or authority over the work that they get done, one who has been assigned to a particular project where the manager or the supervisor is going to be looking just at the end result. They won't necessarily look at how the employee gets it done, just at the result. That's why this kind of evaluation measure can be for an employee as well as an independent contractor.

The last category under the behavioral function is training on the job. If you, as the business owner, provide your worker with training on how to do the job, this is going to be an indication that you, as the business owner, want the job done in a specific way. This again is strong evidence that the worker is an employee, not a contractor.

When you look at periodic or ongoing training about procedures and methods, that's an even stronger evidence of an employer-employee relationship, rather than an entrepreneur or small business owner and contractor relationship. Independent contractors ordinarily use their own methods of getting the job done or learn about the work they're asked to do by doing professional development on their own. They won't be going through you as the business owner for that type of training unless you decide as a small business owner to provide a certain kind of training; but in that case the person is still categorized as an independent contractor, not an employee.

Financial controls

Now let's begin to examine the second common law, which is financial controls. Financial control basically refers to facts that demonstrate that you as an employer have the right to control the economic aspects of the worker's job. Exactly what might that look like? Here are the categories of financial control factors:

- Investments are considered significant
- Expenses are not reimbursed
- Profit or loss is on the table

- Services are offered in the marketplace
- The forms and ways of payments used vary

We will now look at each one of these a little closer, starting with significant investment. Independent contractors, most of the time, invest their own money in the equipment they will use to work with you and to deliver those things that you've contracted them for. However, there are some exceptions to that, particularly in occupations like construction workers, for example. Construction workers typically buy their own equipment, yet they're still classified as employees in that industry. There is no specific dollar limit that contractors are required to meet for it to be considered a significant investment. Additionally, a significant investment is not definitive in determining contractor status, and certain work categories do not require large expenditures; people in these fields don't necessarily spend a lot of money on equipment, but still can be classified as independent contractors.

It is common for independent contractors to have unreimbursed expenses versus those of an employee, because for an employee that brings on expenses, a lot of the time they turn in their paperwork to be reimbursed through expense reports, and often it's already been pre-approved before they go on a trip or work on a project where money has to be spent.

However, at various times an employee can have unreimbursed expenses, depending on the type of services they perform for the company. Those must be a little bit more specific, and if they are unreimbursed then that is a cost that the employee will pick up. If the person is truly categorized correctly as an independent contractor, though, they're typically always unreimbursed expenses.

The final component of financial controls is the opportunity for profit or loss. When a worker has both significant investment in the tools and equipment used and unreimbursed expenses, there is a greater chance to lose money. For example, their expenses may exceed their income from the work. The possibility of taking on loss is a sure sign that the individual is classified as an independent contractor.

Now, for services available to the market, an independent contractor is generally free to seek out other business opportunities, and they don't have to be contracted with just one entrepreneur or small business owner. Independent contractors often advertise and maintain a visible business location and are available to work in the relevant markets. They can work with whomever they choose to work with; therefore, working with multiple clients is a common activity.

Then there is the method of payment. An employee is generally given a regular wage, either hourly, weekly, or monthly. This usually indicates that the worker is an employee, even when the wage or salary is supplemented by a commission, because a commission-based employee is usually a salesperson. An independent contractor, however, is usually paid by a flat fee for the job, or maybe by a retainer, which is another version of a flat fee. However, it is common in some professions, such as the law, to pay independent contractors hourly.

These are the financial control factors you must keep in mind to ensure that you're actually working with a contractor and not an employee. There are several factors, as you can see, that you must be clear about as you determine what support is best for your business.

Type of relationship

The last of the three common laws is the type of relationship. The type of relationship refers to facts that show how the worker and you as the business owner perceive the working relationship. The factors that characterize the type of relationship between two working parties will generally fall into the following:

- Written agreements
- Benefits offered to employees
- Duration of the relationship
- Key business services

Let's talk written contracts. Although the language in a contract can state whether an individual is an independent contractor or an employee, that is not enough to definitively determine the worker's classification. In general, the IRS, which provides guidelines for determining a contractor status, is not responsible for following up and stating whether or not the individual is responsible for paying self-employment tax.

The second factor is the employee benefits, which include things like health insurance, pension plans, paid vacation, sick days, and personal days. Maybe there's disability insurance included, too. It is a general rule in business that independent contractors are not provided benefits; therefore, if you use independent contractors, that can easily be eliminated from your budget. However, the lack of employee-based benefits doesn't definitively label an individual as an independent contractor.

The duration of the relationship is the third factor in characterizing the type of relationship. Whenever you hire a worker and have the expectation of a potential relationship being long-term or indefinite, versus a specific time frame for a project, then the intention will be interpreted and seen as an employer-employee relationship.

The last of the four factors is key business services. If a worker provides services that are considered a core piece of the business, it is more likely that his or her work activities, how things get done and when, will be controlled by the business. For example, if an accounting firm hires a CPA, it is very likely that it will present that CPA's work as its own, thereby having the right to control or direct the work performed. This is a very clear indication that an employer-employee relationship has been formed.

All three of these laws together, the common rules, will help guide you to determine if the person that you have been working with who is categorized as an independent contractor should really be categorized as an employee.

Finding the right person

Now that we've gone through the steps of determining whether you have an employee or an independent contractor, let's talk about where you can find the right person for your business needs. You could start with your own network database and with the professional relationships that you've developed while operating your business; in addition, talk to the people in your online business community to inquire about where they get some of their contractors. Then, of course, there's third party entities like Upwork.com. These three areas—your own network, the network of your professional contacts, and third-party entities—are all great places to begin looking for qualified contractors to work with whatever project or assignment that you would like to give them. They're good areas to start with in tracking down the right kind of contractor that you need.

Just as you would have the proper paperwork in place if you were hiring an employee, you need to have the right forms in place when you begin to contract with individuals that will be serving you in the capacity of an independent contractor. One of the first documents I will suggest to you is an independent contractor agreement. Now, this document basically defines the terms of the agreement, including the duration of time that the contractor will be working for you. It also specifies the deliverables and the end results that you're going to be looking for at the close of the contract, as well as the fees that you and that particular individual have discussed and agreed upon.

The second document is the NDA, or the nondisclo-sure agreement. This document is going to help protect confidentiality and will cover the access your contractor will be given to carry out certain duties and tasks that he or she is contracted to complete. That confidentiality might be about a proprietary material that you have or certain equipment that you may give the contractor ac-cess to. The NDA helps to guard the confidentiality factor of anything that would be proprietary to your company.

The third form I will suggest that you have in place is the W-9. That is the tax information form that will be used to generate a 1099 during tax season. If the indi-vidual earns $600 or more while working with you on the project you contracted them for, you will be required to file with the IRS to have a 1099 generated and sent to the contractor during the following tax season after they've completed work with you.

Those three documents, the independent contractor agreement, the NDA or nondisclosure agreement, and the W-9, will get you started with an independent con-tractor as you go forward.

Finally, we come to closing out the contract. As the deliverables are successfully fulfilled by the contractor, it's important to close out the contract properly, ensuring that all monies owed have been paid in a timely manner and any feedback that should be shared with the contractor is communicated. When you incorporate these steps to building contractor relationships, I'm convinced you will continue to grow in size and revenue in your business as you delegate those things that take you away from building and working on your business.

Employees

Whenever you start hiring employees, it's important to understand that this is a very critical phase in your growth, and although it's an exciting time, it can be equally filled with anxiety. Your company is thriving and growing by leaps and bounds now, and your goal is to establish a payroll-based employee group. What is a payroll-based employee group? It's a group of individuals who will come on board and be committed to your overall vision and mission for growth and expansion over the long term.

In partnering with so many entrepreneurs and small business leaders, I have discovered that many are not always sure when it's the right time to hire. There's a fine line between when it's time to hire or invest in permanent employees versus staying with short-term contracted workers. Before you, as an employer, make these decisions, it's suggested that you analyze your current staff capabilities, their workload, and their efficiency by asking these questions:

1. Do current employees have the right and best tools to get the job done? Without the proper tools in place, there's going to be a difficulty for that employee to get the job done that you were expecting them to do.

2. Does your current staff have the skills to perform at the level demanded of the job? If the demands of the job have risen, have the skill sets of the current employees that you have right now improved?

3. Are the jobs within your company structured correctly?

4. Do you have the right jobs in place, or the right positions in place, to fulfill the demands that you have coming in?

5. Is there an overlap in responsibilities that can be streamlined? Do you have more than one person doing the same job? That's usually what causes redundancy. You'll want to streamline and have everybody in their lane, doing the job that you hired them to do in a way that meets your expectations.

After you answer those questions, the follow-up is then to look at the eight signs that it's a good time to hire; according to Brian Driscoll, district president of Robert Half International, this is what those signs look like:

1. **Growth opportunities are deferred.** You have the financial resources to pursue new business, but any current staff cannot handle the stepped-up workload it would entail to fulfill that new business. So, what do you have to do? You wait instead of growing, and of course growing is

one of the main objectives of any entrepreneur and small business owner.

2. **Acquiring new clients makes you worry.** New business isn't making you smile. Maybe you've contracted new client accounts, but you're not celebrating because you or your team are worrying about how to get it all done. Now a level of anxiety is building up and there are no smiles on your faces.

3. **Even top performers can't keep up.** Communication with your employees is suffering and they're missing deadlines constantly. When there's a breakdown in the communication process, your employees' work can truly suffer, even amongst your top performers.

4. **Overtime is becoming the norm instead of the exception.** Now it's not just around peak seasons or big projects anymore; overtime has become, again, the rule rather than the exception. Work is starting to cross over into your home life. Now, your employees, being understaffed, are taking their anxiety, worry, and stress home to their families, which can cause conflict there.

5. **You're pitching in too often.** Any good manager knows when to roll up his or her sleeves and pitch in, right? But the problem now is that you're doing the work of multiple employees.

That truly is a tell-tell sign you do not have enough employees working for you right now.

6. **Tardiness and absenteeism are on the rise.** Your team has started using any sick days available, and not just to sleep longer; their work overload has started to affect their health. When health is impeded, there is a rise in health care costs, which obviously is going to affect your bottom line on your budget.

7. **Mistakes are happening too often.** In their haste to get a laundry list of work done, more mistakes are being made by the team now than in the past. When asked, the team explains they don't have the time to recheck their work before moving on. When errors are not caught, that can cause even more conflict on the customer side.

8. **Clients are beginning to talk.** Customer expectations are not being met, and they are speaking up more about deadlines not being met, the poor quality of the work being done, and inconsistent communication. You don't want to let everything fall apart and get to that point where clients are noticing. (https://www.ziprecruiter.com/blog/how-to-know-when-its-time-to-hire)

It's important for you to focus and gain clarity about these signs on when it's a good time to hire, even if it's just by one employee.

The pre-hire phase

In the pre-hire phase, creating a budget to hire is key in determining your hiring cost. Within that budgeting, any salary or wage calculated should be marketplace competitive and comparable to the jobs that already exist. Being marketplace competitive increases your chance of attracting higher-quality candidates. You never want to be too cheap, nor over-price a job.

Another part of the pre-hire phase is a well-written job description that clearly identifies the skills and experience required and the tasks and responsibilities of that role. A job description also helps you to identify your expectations about the job for the prospective employee. If you have an employee in place but no job description has been defined for them, that makes it a little bit more difficult for that person to understand what it is that you are wanting them to do and what your expectations are for that job. A written job description is always critical in your business.

You will want to pay attention to ensure you have the tools in place that the employee would need to utilize to perform his or her job duties. For example, make sure their computer, phone, and other office essentials are in place, particularly if the employee would be on site with you. This may even apply if the employee is a person who telecommutes or works virtually for you, because you may choose to have a phone or computer supplied for them that they use.

In the previous segment I talked about having a job description in place in the pre-hire phase. There are specific components that should be in any job description that you write:

- Have a job title
- Identify a reporting supervisor or manager
- Assign a job code
- Include the job classification (hourly, non-exempt, or salaried exempt)
- What do I mean by a job code? This is a reference that is created by individual companies for organizational purposes. Say, for instance, you are hiring a marketing coordinator. The job code could be specific to your company's name or it could be specific to the department. If it's a marketing coordinator, you could say MKC10591. So, that means Marketing Coordinator, and the job number that is assigned to that job is 10591. You can begin creating your own sequences of job codes as you begin to hire on more employees.

Other components of a good job description include:

- Write a short company overview or brief synopsis of your company and what you do
- List the tasks and responsibilities for the job
- Include compensation information, both pay and benefits; everyone wants to know what they will be paid

- Identify key qualifications and skills that are required to perform the job

- Insert an EEOC nondiscrimination statement. For example, "we do not discriminate against age, sex, race, religion, ethnicity, disability, and national origin"

When you get to the hiring phase, have a copy of the job description on hand to have your new employee review. Include a blank for a signature and date at the end of the job description. This confirms that the employee received the job description and understands it; have them sign off on it and put the date of confirmation. Keep a copy in their employee personnel files.

The recruiting and hiring phase

After you have written your job description, you're ready to send out your job ad. You can extract some information from the job description to create your job ad. Once you've done that, you can begin posting it on various job posting sites. Some of these sites you will need to pay a minimal cost to use, and some are free. Some examples of job posting sites are Monster.com, Indeed. com, SimplyHired.com, FlexJobs.com (which, by the way, is a great one for telecommuters), and Craig's List.

Other options that bring you more into the twenty-first century, if you will, include Facebook, Twitter, LinkedIn, Pinterest, Instagram, Snapchat, and Periscope. There's a vast number of platforms where you can place a job ad and capture the attention of great potential employees.

From there, it's time to set up your email for resume submissions. I would suggest that, similarly to the way you set up for internship applications, you set up a simple Gmail account and make it separate from your business account so you won't be inundated in your inbox. All the resumes would just go to that Gmail account, and that's the only reason that you would use that account, to capture those resumes.

After the resumes are submitted and received, begin to prescreen those resumes and narrow them down to pre-qualified candidates to begin pre-screen calls. You want to narrow it down to the top three to six candidates that you've chosen from the prescreen resumes. Following your prescreening process, you're then able to set up direct interviews, which leads you to choosing the number one and best fit person that you want to extend an official offer to. These steps are a snapshot of the recruiting and hiring phase that you're going to take to secure a hire.

As with every hire, there are required documents. One last thing to have in order is your personnel files, where you want to store the documents associated with the hire. In those required documents, you should have a completed employment application, a copy of the applicant's resume, and tax forms. Those tax forms include a state income tax form as well as a federal W-4 unless you're in a state with a flat income tax. For instance, North Carolina and Georgia are a couple of examples of states that require you to pay state income taxes as well. You will also need to include an I-9 Employment Eligibility form for your personnel file. This form ensures that the individual is eligible to work in the United States; you are required to have an I-9 Eligibility Form on file for any employee that you hire. Other forms will include a bank authorization form for them if you will be paying through automatic deposits, or ACH deposits as they're typically called.

Something else I would encourage you to have is an employee handbook that includes an acknowledgement form. If you have a policy book—and you should have one in place—then at the end of that there would be an acknowledgement form where the employee signs off on it, saying that they did receive it. Now, it doesn't guarantee that they're going to read it, but it does guarantee that they have received the employee handbook; after that, of course, it's up to them to read it.

Now that you've successfully come through the recruiting and hiring part of this process, the last step of the process is onboarding. The onboarding process really should take more than just a day. Allow me to take you back to your corporate days. Remember on your first day? That's typically your orientation day. An HR rep came into the room with you and several other people who may have started on the same day as you. They gave you a stack of paperwork, and you went through the paperwork, completed it, and gave it back to the HR rep so they could begin to set up your personnel file. Then, they directed you to the department that you needed to report to with your supervisor or manager. That supervisor or manager may have talked to you for a couple of minutes, and then they threw you in a cubicle or office and told you to get to work. Does any of that sound familiar?

Well, a truly effective onboarding process can be established in thirty-, sixty-, or ninety-day increments. Of course, it is up to you as a business owner how long that onboarding process will be, but I strongly encourage that you make it at least thirty days to really, truly set that new hire up for success.

What are some of the things that you can do as part of the onboarding process? Of course, you should introduce the new hire to any employees that are already in place. Let them know right away who they are and how they will be part of the team, and what part they're going to be playing. Then you want to meet with your new hire to discuss your expectations. Now this is very critical. This is probably one of the most important conversations you're going to have in the beginning with this new hire, because they need to understand what your expectations are when it comes to them fulfilling their responsibilities for the role that you hired them to work in. That really will be one of your most critical conversations that you will have. Again, set them up for success from the beginning.

You want to ask them if they have any questions you can clear up for them at that time. They'll be able to give you feedback if something is not clear. It's important to establish those guidelines right off the bat. Show them where they're going to be working, what kind of environment it is. Talk a little bit more about the company, and go more in depth about the culture and how things flow there. You may even want to let them know where to go have lunch, take their breaks, or hang their coat up. You really want to welcome them in and let them know they are a part of the culture and part of the company now. These are just a few suggestions that you can have as part of the onboarding process; I will go into more detail about onboarding in a later chapter.

Define who will fit your business culture

As you go through the process of recruiting and onboarding a team for your business, one of the characteristics to consider is if the individuals possess the character and knowledge that aligns with what you have defined as your business culture.

In chapter 2 I broke down culture and provided a blueprint to understanding it and how to begin implementing it in your own business, no matter your size. With that blueprint you are better able to identify an individual who fits the culture without it being forced. Through the interview process, asking questions, getting feedback, checking their background, and even watching their body language all should help you conclude whether he or she does align and would be an asset.

EVERY She-EO needs this book! Created for a Mastermind by a Mastermind! HR is Sexy! Every She-EO needs to have this book for quick reference and research. This is the perfect blueprint, providing step-by-step directions on how to properly SCALE, GROW, and EXPAND your business. It's time for us to shift our thinking. HR is Sexy! And being HR compliant is the sexiest thing you can do for the future of your business.

Nicole Gates, Founder
Gates Uncorked Lifestyle
www.gatesuncorkedtravelntours.agency

CHAPTER 6

Hiring a Kick-Ass Team

Setting the rhythm for hiring

Hiring, as mentioned in previous chapters, can cause anxiety when it is not part of your normal daily routine, and especially when it's not something you have ever done before as an entrepreneur. We all know that as entrepreneurs, our biggest focus is usually around securing clients and generating money. However, without putting some key mechanisms in place, the money that's coming in can quickly shift in the other direction. As with most business activities, a pattern or rhythm develops the more you do it, and it almost becomes second nature. Hiring is no different, in that there is a rhythm in doing it more effectively. There is a methodology to it, and Topgrading is one worth exploring.

As defined and developed by authors Brad and Geoff Smart, Topgrading is a method of recruiting, interviewing, selecting, and retaining top talent. It was designed to increase your likelihood of hiring and retaining A Players when used in conjunction with what's called job scorecards. When I was first reading about this method, I realized that I was already very familiar with its concepts; it's a method I will be using more in my own consulting practice as I help more and more small business clients build their core A-team. You ask, what is a job scorecard? Essentially, the scorecard sets expectations around KPIs (key performance indicators) and expected results. It can also serve as the framework to rate performance and be used as a coaching document that helps identify opportunities for ongoing development and improvement. Use it quarterly, annually, or whenever there is a need to have a conversation about performance with one of your employees. With job scorecards, you can better attract and retain the A Players you need to hit your growth goals.

Taking into consideration the overall concept of Topgrading and the message it conveys to acquire top employment, here is my own take on it:

1. **Define for your own business what an "A Player" looks like.** Look for someone who rises to the top of the talent pool for key positions. Generally, that level of a candidate will easily fall within the top 10 percent. Jack Welch said it best: "an A Player will not only be able to consistently deliver good results but will also do it in a way that is aligned with your core values." You as a CEO leader will have to apply the definition you choose; however, the other key is to ensure that you've conveyed your expectations to everyone involved in the recruitment of and search for the best-fit talent, resulting in everyone being on the same page.

2. **Create your job scorecards.** This is the tool that helps you define the purpose behind your top talent search, the skills, competencies, responsibilities, and values you use to apply an evaluation. Not only will it be important to create job scorecards during the recruiting and hiring phases, implementing such an approach throughout the company for all staff members will also establish a more cohesive working environment. When everyone is clear on their roles and on the expectations of the company and the direction it's going, the business can have a greater impact in the market.

3. **Identify internal A Players or employees already showing signs of being one.** Based on how you define a top-tier employee candidate, assess who's already on your current team. More often than not, there are rock star employees who have already bought into the mission and vision of the business. The ultimate goal would be to have an office full of rock stars; however, I don't have to tell you that most companies don't realistically possess that ideal scenario. But this simply gives you a baseline to improve upon over time.

Now that we have examined the above three elements of defining what your top player will be, the next steps are all about the weeding out process known as interviewing.

1. Start with your own circle.

2. Implement a series of interviews.

3. A pre-screen interview to start the elimination phase

4. A direct interview with focus on competencies

5. A knock-out round of interviews

6. Determine if it's a good match.

I realize that you may not be quite ready for such an intense level of interviewing; however, you should see it as a blueprint for attracting the right people to your business as you continue to grow over the coming months and years. If you're interested in learning more details about these steps, or in learning more about Topgrading in general, you can find more information at https://www.topgrading.com or in *Topgrading: How to Hire, Coach, and Keep A Players* by Brad and Geoff Smart.

Delmar is absolutely fantastic. My wife owns a small bakery in metro Atlanta (www.ALSHbakery.com or www.ALSHstore.com) which she started in 2010. We hired Delmar to help us find the right part-time baker to hire. Delmar provided big corporation human resources to our small bakery at a reasonable cost. From posting the job to screening the applicants, Delmar helped us find the right hire. She also helped us with transitioning the employee into our business. We love our part-time baker. We will certainly work with Delmar in the future.

Thomas & Melanie Wideman
A Little Slice of Heaven Bakery
https://alshbakery.com

CHAPTER 7

Onboarding Your Team for Success

What is onboarding all about?

Onboarding can be viewed as part orientation and part employee success track. Before I dive into the onboarding process, allow me to tell you a little story.

Imagine this: you have a job candidate who has done all the right things to ensure he or she has successfully gotten through the hiring process, including a series of interviews that allowed them to sell themselves on the knowledge, skills, and abilities you were in search of as an employer. Now the initial recruiting is over, and your rock star new hire is ready to start.

Fast forward to the day your new hire begins. They come through the doors with great enthusiasm to do their best and, of course, make the best first impression possible. But here's the gag. Your new employee is ready to meet the team and get straight to work, but their impression of you as an employer is not quite what they were hoping. No one greets the new hire at the door, no one from management shows up to give direction on where to go, nor is it clear to any of the current staff that a new person was starting. Did that make your radar go up about how you as the employer play a significant part in setting up your new hire for successful acclimation from day one?

Let's continue. After they get past their immediate disappointment, they are then pointed to the hiring manager, who is too busy in a meeting to take up the baton, say hello, and find out how things are going, and who proceeds to brush the new hire off to a supervisor who is even less prepared to jumpstart the day, because no plans had been made.

Your new hire finally makes it to their desk and sits in silence, trying to figure out where to start on their own or who to ask amongst the team about how they can help. At this point, figuring out what the company is all about or what kind of values are running through the veins of the work environment almost seems ridiculous. Just getting the opportunity to start with even the simplest of tasks is all they really want to do.

The hope is that by the next day, or at the very least the next week, things will turn around with a second impression. Whoever said there is no second time to make a first impression never talked to a bright-eyed rock star of a new hire who remains determined to show off the reasons you hired them.

That's the kind of experience to intentionally avoid giving a new hire at all costs with your business and brand. As an employer, I thought that would be a great story to start with, to really set the tone of this topic and put you in the mindset of why it is so important to have a proper onboarding process for your business.

Finding the best candidate to join your company is a big deal in building the right team, but it's not the only thing. The opportunity to set up a new hire for success is equally as important. This is where the onboarding process comes in, and it plays a critical role in ensuring your new employee is productive and finds their place inside your workplace culture.

However, it has been my experience that in some companies, onboarding is seen as orientation. Orientation is necessary, because paperwork and other routine tasks must be done administratively; however, onboarding is more about having the new talent become acclimated to the workplace culture, your business personality, and their new role. It involves management, as well as other employees, to help the transition, and can last up to twelve months. The general rule of thumb for onboarding is ninety days; however, if we're honest, one full year would be ideal to have a good feel for how your new employee works and to be assured that they are completely committed to the company's vision.

Before jumping head-first into creating a more standardized onboarding program, there are some questions you must ask:

- What will the parameters be?
- What is an appropriate length of time for effective acclimation?
- What do you want new hires to walk away with?
- Who will be on the onboarding team?

- Who will be charged with tracking their progress?

- What are the goals to be accomplished during the onboarding period?

- How will you capture information on the pros and cons of the process?

One of the most important things you're going to be doing prior to onboarding is considering the costs of hiring. These include things like placing job ads, labor costs, salary, and benefits, as well as the time you spent focused on hiring and interviewing potential applicants. Then there's the cost to replace an employee who leaves the company. You must keep all these things in mind about what it is that you need to do as a business owner before you move into an onboarding process.

According to a study of over a thousand people done by BambooHR, 31 percent of respondents had quit a job within six months of starting it (BambooHR Employee Survey, https://www.bamboohr.com/blog/onboarding-infographic). In addition, a steady stream of employees left after the first week all the way up to the third month. Within the study, new hires identified what they really wanted from their first week, and the statistics were very telling: first, 76 percent of those new hires said that on-the-job training was most important to them. That's followed up by 73 percent who wanted a review of company policies, because it was important for them to know what the expectations were and what the job culture was about.

The next percentage was 59 percent, which related to new employees wanting to take a company tour and review equipment setup and procedures. The study was rounded out with 56 percent wishing they had had a buddy or a mentor through that first month or two. They wanted to learn how to do their job and understand the inner workings of the company. In short, they wanted to start doing meaningful work and contribute fast.

These are some of the effects of onboarding—because there's such a thing as bad and good in an onboarding process. Results of a bad onboarding process can include such things as:

- Loss of a quality employee because no expectations were communicated, nor guidance provided to better understand their job.

- Need for oversight of bad hires because not enough attention was given to evaluate their work. Have you heard the phrase "hire slow, fire fast"? I say it all the time when I'm teaching entrepreneurs how to effectively hire.

- Loss of productivity from the new hire because their initial ramping up was less than perfect. Or, equally comparable, an ineffective onboarding process causes the new hire to produce less due to stress and feeling overwhelmed.

None of these are good places to start. These are all things I want to help you try to avoid. To retain your new hires, the key will be a structured and planned-out onboarding process that pinpoints the element of success at each phase of the process. This will include communicating your expectations and your company's value system.

It may seem as though it's not such a big deal up front, letting a few hires slip through the cracks; however, that is the gateway to setting a subpar standard to building a team, and can lead to a business that doesn't have the impact that you have imagined in the marketplace of competitors. Never have the attitude that there's not enough resources or time to implement a process that ensures fairness and the opportunity to be trained and developed. You as a business owner may not feel like you have the time or resources to spend, but that means you also don't have the time or resources to lose. You really don't want to be in a losing position.

When respondents of the Bamboo HR survey were asked what would have helped them stay at a job, there were two things that stood out: 23 percent of respondents said receiving clear guidelines as to what their responsibilities were would have helped, and 21 percent said they wanted more effective training. It's very important for you to have clear guidelines of what it is that you want your new hires to do, and that your new hires are clear about what you want them to do. Equally as important, you want to offer them the opportunity to learn as they grow with your company. A developed team is a direct reflection of what you value as an employer.

Informal versus formal onboarding

I thought it would be a good idea to do some comparison of what an informal onboarding process looks like versus a more formal process. What does an informal process look like? A new hire comes in on their first day and you introduce him or her to the team. You give the tour if you have a brick and mortar, or you hop on a video meeting with them if you have a virtual work environment. You may assign a few tasks to get them started. Then you return to doing your own work.

The problem with that scenario is that the new hire is basically left to their own devices to figure out what's next. It doesn't take long for the employee to complete the initial tasks you gave them. They start wondering what else they can do. You have nothing to direct them to and decide to hand the employee off to a direct supervisor. The quandary with that decision is that neither the manager nor the supervisor have discussed a game plan to give the new hire a more structured onboarding experience. To avoid starting the new hire down the wrong path because of your unpreparedness, take a step back and regroup with a game plan. In doing so, you avoid wasting time and money.

What are some better options? To avoid those types of scenarios mentioned, you want to take your onboarding process personally. What does that really mean? You want to create an atmosphere that feels welcoming to your new hire. Have their paperwork ready to sign and be able to explain it to them. Have their workstation ready; or, if they're not at a workstation at a brick and mortar, have a computer or telephone ready for them if they're going to be assigned these items, and if not, have their password, login information, and all those types of things prepared. Lay out your expectations of what you want out of them. You can have a plan beyond day one that incorporates a thirty-, sixty-, or ninety-day roadmap, because onboarding goes far beyond just the first day. Perhaps you want to implement a checklist process, as checklists are always good and help you stay on track with what you're doing.

To jumpstart you in creating your own onboarding process, whether it's over the course of thirty days or longer, I've provided a recommended checklist of steps that will assist you in staying on track in effectively acclimating your new hires.

Before the new hire's first day on the job, here are some suggested things you could do:

- After the new employee confirms their acceptance, officially welcome him or her on a telephone call.

- Provide the new employee with a contact in the event of a question or issue that may come up, especially one that you're not able to address immediately, but you have a point person that can.

- Create an onboarding schedule for the new employee.

- Schedule the new employee to attend new employee orientation. Again, it's more than just one day of orientation. It really should be encompassing the scope and time-frame of the entire process as well.

- Set up a computer, phone, login, password, and office supplies, whether you have an offline or online business.

- Send an announcement via email to your team, if you already have a team in place, announcing the new hire and when they will start.

These are what some first-day activities could be for your new hire:

- Communicate with your new hire on setting expectations and introducing objectives.

- Instruct the new hire to complete new hire forms.

- Introduce them to any coworkers or team members that you may already be working with.

- Review their work schedule and pay schedule. People always want to know when they should be at work, what their typical work schedule is, and when they're scheduled to get paid.

- Provide computer orientation at their desk. Maybe there's an opportunity to walk them through what their login information is, as well as passwords and things that they need to know, such as if there's shared drives on a network that you may have, email logins for shared accounts, those types of things. If you have an online business, you can still walk them through this remotely.

- Arrange a welcome lunch for the new employee. If you have a virtual employee, maybe you can send them to lunch and pay for their lunch ahead of time at their favorite place.

What could the first week look like for your new hire? You can review their job responsibilities. They want to know what they're supposed to be doing, and what your expectations are—which was what 23 percent of respondents on the statistic we looked at earlier said would've helped.

Review your company's mission, what your strategy is, your values, how you function as a company, and your policies and procedures. Again, these are just examples. You might make sure they're aware of critical members of the team, if you already have a team, what your company calendar is, or some things that are coming up that you want them to be involved in. You can go over confidentiality of information, emergency regulations, and any health and safety training, if that's part of your business. You want to review the company's training courses, if that's applicable to what you do as a business owner. Then, schedule weekly or monthly meetings to touch base with your new hire. Again, we're talking about a thirty-, sixty-, or ninety-day rule of thumb for an effective onboarding process to really take place and to really, truly be implemented.

Now, what could the first month look like? Or the first ninety days, or the first six months? The first month could be ensuring that a new hire enrolls in benefits, if that's applicable to your business, within thirty days of their first day of employment. The supervisor, if there's a supervisor you have assigned, should review and clarify performance objectives and expectations after their first month, after they've been in the atmosphere long enough to get some semblance of what's going on in the culture of the business.

During the first ninety days, review and discuss the team member's performance objectives and what you're going to be measuring their performance on over the course of the next six to twelve months. Then, at the six-month period, again review performance objectives.

Discuss training they have completed, whether the training was given by your company or was from attending a seminar, for example. The more equipped and more learned your team is, the better it is for you. It brings even more value to your business.

Lastly, as your company grows, the onboarding process may need to shift some. You may maintain some of the standard parts of an onboarding process; however, depending on how big your company grows through different development stages, you will want to adjust your onboarding process accordingly.

Creating a winning experience

A winning experience will be a two-way street. As much as it's essential to set your new hire up to win, it's just as important for that same new hire to get in tune with your leadership style. The more you are empowered in demonstrating how you operate, the more your new hire knows what to expect in how their zone of genius can work well within your business culture. After the traditional timeframe of onboarding, the process then moves more into retention and shifts from on-the-job training to continuous development.

PART IV

TRANSITIONING FROM ENTREPRENEUR TO CEO

CHAPTER 8

The CEO Shift Every Entrepreneur Must Make

Why is a shift in mindset necessary and non-negotiable?

It's been said that for anything to change, it must first happen in your mind. And one of the biggest changes or shifts you can make in business is becoming the chief executive officer. As the head of your business, you are the one seen as the leader and visionary of a concept that others buy into through their commitment to work with you and for you; for that to happen, a mindset shift is required.

In order to grow, you must shift from working *in* the business to working *on* the business to truly transition your mindset to that of a CEO. As an entrepreneur, your mindset very likely may have been to pull yourself up by your bootstraps as you handle any and all tasks that might be necessary, like graphics, social media, and blogs; however, the CEO mindset invests in bringing on higher-level positions and trusts their team members to make strategic, not just tactical, moves.

Here are a few suggested steps you can begin to take to transition into thinking and acting more like a CEO:

1. **CEOs hold the vision of the business instead of being the implementers**

   Ask yourself: are you the one that gets things done, no matter what? There's nothing wrong with being a CEO that gets things done, but is that the best use of your time, being caught up in the day-to-day operations? You are the visionary. You need to be the one that helps others see what you see while also understanding what it will take to accomplish those things and grow.

2. **CEOs are very good at simplifying things that are deemed complicated**

   Yes, as entrepreneur leaders we are always thinking of ideas and ways to improve and grow our businesses. But do you find yourself ever limiting or blocking your imagination? To be what's considered a successful CEO, work on containing your ideas and visions to the point where you can lay them out on the table in the simplest form so that your team can pick them up and implement them effectively. If you assume that using overcomplicated strategies and business jargon is how a business leader demonstrates their position as a CEO, you will inevitably lose the commitment of your team.

3. **CEOs are clear about what they want and how to get it**

   If you are seeking input from too many outside sources, or even too much input from your own executive management team, needing validation about what you should be doing, STOP; you are headed down the wrong path. You must have clarity and surety about what you want if being successful as a CEO is the goal. A CEO mindset will not be circling the drain of what to do or not do. Rather, you will tap into the "delegation" side of your thinking and empower your team to get the job done.

4. **CEOs accept that responsibility falls squarely on their shoulders**

   In corporate standards, it's usually a board of directors that will give a CEO his or her marching orders. The board may guide or outline steps they believe would be best; however, you as the CEO must have a mindset that accepts accountability and takes responsibility for having oversight over all aspects of the company. No matter the circumstances, a successful CEO should never play the blame game. With that being said, if a CEO is who you are, you must be prepared to take control of the company's reins and be ready to take the blows and the blame, while still forging ahead with the vision.

5. **CEOs are very good at delegating**

   Delegation is a key ingredient in being a successful CEO. You can't be afraid to let go of some control and delegate to your team, the one that you've filled with skilled and capable individuals. The opposite of delegation is micromanaging, and that should never be a part of your equation if you're to be an effective CEO. As a CEO, you will depend on your direct subordinates, like the CFO and COO, and other department heads to delegate down the hierarchy to get things done every day. To evolve into the CEO you want to be, you will have to make the decision to "fire yourself" and entrust others to carry the vision forward.

Growing occurs in a field of possibility

As you look toward becoming a successful CEO, you must begin by laying the foundation. Stephen Covey, the author of *Seven Habits of Highly Effective People*, once said, "Begin with the end in mind." Think of it like this: you didn't become a business leader to struggle through each day trying to achieve your professional goals and have a life. You became a business leader because you have talent. You have skills. You wanted to run the show. You wanted to take control of your career and life and, yes, to make money of course. Why, then, do most small business leaders seem to struggle? That is because the leap to thinking and acting like a CEO is not always the easiest shift.

As a result, many of you are wearing yourselves out as you continually put out fires. You jump on the next great revenue opportunity, and you try to do everything yourself, which is almost virtually impossible. Instead, try to apply what Stephen Covey said: "Begin with the end in mind." Think of where you want your vision to go, where you want your business to go, and then figure out the steps to get there. Reverse engineer it and determine the steps to take until you reach where you are right now. How do you get to that thing that's at the end, that is the result of what you're wanting to achieve?

What's your legacy? Have you given much thought to that? A legacy is defined as the sum of all the outcomes resulting from our behavior that others continue to remember about us. It's not a strategic plan that can be nicely quantified and measured; it's something that gets handed down. What are we talking about when we talk about legacy? If you want to develop a CEO mindset, you need to think about what kind of legacy you want to leave.

Here are several elements that paint a basic picture of what a legacy could be. Of course, your legacy could be many things; maybe you have not yet defined what your legacy is going to be for yourself or your business, but hopefully this will get your creative juices flowing to really think about what your legacy should be. Is your legacy your work contributions? Is it what you do in your business, the products and services that you offer? How you make other people's lives easier with what it is that you offer through your brand and through your business? Is it something that you're doing in your community to make a difference in other people's lives? Are you educating them? Are you equipping them to be in new careers? Are you equipping them to go to whatever level of success that they have in their own minds and from their own perspective?

Your legacy could be the impact that you make upon your children. Well, maybe you don't have any children, that's quite all right, but it could be other children that are in the world that you're making an impact on. It could be your family, whether that be your own personal family or people you mentor who have become like family. How are you serving on a global scale? Are you thinking beyond the four walls that you're in? Are you thinking beyond the community that you're in? Begin to give great thought to what your legacy should be as a leader in your own business. Again, as Stephen Covey notes, you must begin with the end in mind. So ask yourself, what is your legacy? What do you want to be remembered for?

Take inventory of yourself. Socrates once said, "the unexamined life is not worth living." When is the last time you examined who you are and examined your life? Every year, most successful CEOs take inventory and create strategic plans for the coming year, not only for their organizations but also for themselves. Why? As leaders, they know it's important to plan for their own development as well as that of their organization. They take a critical look at both their assets and liabilities, creating a personal balance or scorecard for themselves.

In his book *Good to Great: Why Some Companies Make the Leap . . . and Others Don't*, Bill Collins indicates that level five leaders, those that do whatever is needed to be done to make the company great, also exhibit extreme personal humility within intense professional will. As leaders, they look outside themselves when something goes well and look at themselves when things go wrong. So, you as a leader need to take accountability for yourself and your own actions. You take accountability for what's going right and wrong in your business. When times are tough—and who doesn't have an experience of challenges and tough days sometimes—the most successful leaders don't fall victim to the impulse to lay blame. As a leader, what do you do? You take ownership. You take ownership of whatever tough time is occurring. Sometimes you must correct your course when challenges come up or when you're trying to meet those challenges. It's fine to have to make those course corrections, but it's also important to take on ownership of the previous course. You must take the time to examine your life as a leader.

Delmar Johnson is an amazing asset to any company looking to recruit, grow, and retain a rock star team. Her experience and genuine passion for helping companies thrive made working with her an absolute pleasure. Not only did she assist with HR and recruiting during my fragile startup years, she also helped me grow and transform as a leader. Working with her saved me time and thousands of dollars in mistakes and expenses, and provided me with the confidence to build a solid team. Her willingness to educate me on what I needed at each stage of growth was priceless, and I will always be grateful for the support and the relationship that we have built together. Delmar helped us structure our internship program and grow our team from three interns and one part-time employee to over ten contractors, a management team, and a virtual apprenticeship program to support other emerging entrepreneurs.

Tierra Reid, CEO
TDR Brands International, LLC
www.tierradestinyreid.com

CHAPTER 9

Get Your Business in Order

❧

Creating organization in your business

Entrepreneurs and small business owners are often so busy grinding it out to make things happen that they forget to write down what it is that they are actually doing on a daily basis to make those deals, take care of their customers, build relationships, and so much more. It helps to get organized to know exactly what it is that we as entrepreneurs and small business owners do on an everyday basis.

Identify what you do and how you run your business

Create a system or a process that could essentially allow others to run your business without you even being there; for example, if you go on vacation, have a family emergency, or have something that you need to do that is outside the scope of doing business on any particular day. When you have your systems in place, such as having a list of standard operating procedures, it makes it so much easier for those who are on your team to continue the everyday business operations without you physically being there. Wouldn't that be ideal?

Delmar Johnson

In a nutshell, being without systems is the problem and operational procedures are the solutions. Why do you need an operations manual? First, it helps you to create efficiency in your business and gain a better-trained team and staff when you have procedures and policies in place; it makes it easier to scale your business and to make it more valuable. Second, written processes ensure everyone knows what expectations you've set for your business, so everyone starts off on the same page. It ensures that all new hires are given the same information to help create consistency across the board. Being an HR professional from the corporate sector, and bringing that skillset into the small business community, I've had many discussions with people who have built their team or are in the middle of building their team, but don't have a plan in place of how to help create consistency in their business among their team, or how to continue professional development through the opportunities of training. When there's no plan to help build up your business and your team, then that puts you in a very precarious position.

The third reason why you need an operations manual is that it makes it easier to scale your business. When operating from multiple locations, especially if you have a brick and mortar or you're thinking about franchising a concept you may have, it's impossible to deliver on your brand promise without a comprehensive operational plan in place. Don't get intimidated by the words operations systems or processes and procedures. I'm here to make it a little less intimidating, and you don't have to do this by yourself.

The fourth reason why you need an operations manual is to make your business more valuable. It will be proof that there is an actual business going on, something that can run, again, with or without you being physically present. When you have those kinds of systems in place, people can continue your operations, continue answering the phone for when customers and clients call in and you're not there. They're able to go back and make sure that they're following the steps that you've established in your operational procedures.

Create an operations manual

Typically, in an operations manual, you're going to include your company mission statement, explain what that is, and talk about your company values. Your company values, of course, are the core of what you should be building your business on, whether it's integrity, innovation, creativity, fun, great customer service, great communications, or other core company values. I talked about these previously back in chapter 2.

You should have an organizational chart for a visual of how your team currently looks and how it can look in the future. If you've been in corporate America, you may have previously seen what an organizational chart looks like. You also want to have a chart of your business section, which includes finance, marketing, accounting, and bookkeeping activities.

The most important thing to keep in mind is that it should be useful. If not, it won't be used by anyone, maybe not even by yourself. Start with the information that you would need to reference the most and would like to keep handy. That's where checklists are going to be of use.

Your operations manual should have a contact list; that can include all your employees, or it can include everyone that's on your team, whether those are interns, contractors, or employees, or even if there is an area where you use volunteers sometimes. But whoever is on your team, whoever is helping you carry out your vision, your mission, your goals, and your core values for the business and brand that you have, you're going to want a list of them.

You're going to want a list of your vendors. Who do you go to that helps support you in fulfilling whatever project, task, or responsibilities that you have to fulfill a client's request or the contract that you have with a client? Figure out who you need to fulfill your deliverables, to meet what your agreement has laid out that you will complete for that client. That will include vendors and maybe a graphic designer; it could be someone who handles social media and helps you develop social media strategies. It could be a slew of people who you may reach out to who help to complete an assignment for a customer or a client.

You can have a list of emergency numbers. These would be emergency numbers where people can get ahold of you or get ahold of the exact person or other organization that they need. Whatever your emergency numbers are, someone should be able to look at that emergency number list and be able to pull out the number that they need at any time. You can have your insurance company information in there, too.

If you have a brick and mortar, you don't necessarily own the building you're working in; you may be leasing the building. Now, obviously there's nothing wrong with that. Most brick and mortars are leased or rented. But if you are leasing, you will have a landlord, so you want the landlord information in your operations manual.

Another thing to include in your operations manual is a series of checklists. Not everyone is going to need every checklist, depending on what their position in the company is, but they should be available and in a place everyone knows how to find. For example, if you have a brick and mortar, you'll want to have a checklist of what cleaning your onsite location pertains. So how do you want it cleaned? You want the trash taken out, but do you want the mirrors cleaned? Do you want the computers wiped down? Whatever it is that you have at your onsite location, you need a cleaning checklist.

Something else that requires a checklist is how you open and close your business. What are the supplies that you must get ready and the supplies that you use? Think of what other tasks require easy and repeatable steps to follow. This should get you thinking about what it is that you should have in your operations manual, and creating checklists is a good place to start.

You can also create how-to guides. For instance, if you have a physical location, what do you do if the cash register crashes? How do you fix it? How do you continue to operate, to make sure that a customer is taken care of, if the computer crashes while someone's standing there? Someone needs to be able to access that how-to guide quickly and figure out how to handle things when a cash register goes down. Or what if one of your team members, one of your employees, calls out sick? Well, who's going to back that person up? Is it going to be you, or will it be an additional staff member that's going to come in? Are they going to be on call? Or, in another scenario, what if an employee or a customer gets injured in your store?

Many of these things apply to you even if you have a virtual business. I may be referring to brick and mortar businesses in the examples, but if you have a virtual business, there are similar situations that would trigger what you need to write as part of your operations manual. You want to make a checklist of how the phones are answered, how to handle customers or clients, how to follow up with your customer, and how to close a deal. If you have a virtual assistant or another virtual-type staff member or team member that's helping you with your business operations, you need to know what to do if they call out sick, too, right? Think about how you can apply those same examples in your virtual business.

Make customer service a priority

I want to encourage you to get your customer service policies written down as a priority, because customer service really is the heartbeat of any business, no matter the size of the business. Stellar customer service is what keeps your current customers happy and what helps to attract others to you as potential leads that will hopefully, eventually, turn into a paying client.

Identify different payment methods. Whether you have a brick and mortar or a virtual business, you have different payment methods. Some examples of those different payment methods could be Moonclerk, Business PayPal, Square, or any number of other ways that you can take payments, along with more traditional methods such as cash, checks, and credit or debit cards. Whether you're onsite, offsite, virtual, at a conference, doing a workshop, doing a speaking gig, or wherever it is that you are, you should be able to use those different payment methods. But you have to list what those payment methods are and how to handle a customer transaction in whatever payment method that you use in your business. Your team members also need to understand how to give a refund to a client that may be dissatisfied or want to cancel a contract, as well as knowing how to give a refund back to a person that initially invested in your business as a client or customer. You want to have those policies written down so everyone will understand how to give the money back properly.

Manage your team well

Never do you ever feel as much of a CEO as when you have a team of your own, a group of individuals who made a conscious decision to invest their skills, talent, and knowledge into fulfilling the goals and objectives you have set for running a successful business. As you make the effort to manage your team well, there are some specific actions that will help you establish a standard in doing so:

1. **Define their role.** You want to define each employee's role through a tool like a job description, right? And that job description lets them know exactly what it is that you want them to do. It defines their key responsibilities as well as the qualifications and skillset they should have in order to perform those tasks. Basically, a job description provides a summary of tasks and/ or behaviors the individual will perform and is accountable for in their specific job role.

2. **Coach on the go.** It's important to talk to your employees. Talk to your team about specific behaviors that you see and that you like. Many times, employers become so focused on the behaviors that they don't want to see that they forget to acknowledge the behaviors that are more in alignment with what they do prefer to see. It's best to talk about specific behaviors that you see happening with your employees that you re-

ally like. But then, you also want to have the opportunity when you're coaching on the go to discuss those areas of opportunities to improve. To improve on certain behaviors, you want to be able to balance out that conversation by including what you don't and you do want to see.

3. **Give your undivided attention.** I worked for a big corporation back in the day, and my manager at that time had a great strategy for keeping up with her team. Each one of us on her team had a day when we talked to her about what was going on with our projects and what was going on in the city that we supported. I happened to be in Dallas, Texas, for this company. Individually, we would each give an update on what was going on, such as what kinds of communications occurred from week to week. She assigned each of us a day and a particular hour on her calendar where we were scheduled to have an open dialogue about what was going on. Think about applying that kind of communications in your own business, because it creates an opportunity for dialogue and an open-door policy.

4. **Evaluate their performance more than once a year.** As a consultant, I often encourage clients to evaluate their team's performance throughout the course of the year. At the very minimum, conduct evaluations at least twice

per year. When you get to the end of the year, the progress of your employees' performance is more evident because you conducted those evaluations quarterly or biannually. It's not a one size fits all. Some businesses have a time set aside once a year for looking at performances. Some have twice a year. The most important aspect of any evaluation, however, is to have an ongoing dialogue throughout the year.

5. **Recognize desired behaviors.** If there are certain behaviors that you see going on with someone on your team that are really adding value to what they do, improving how well they produce results that you're looking for, and/or inspiring a great attitude that helps to create a great workplace environment, then that's definitely a time you want to recognize those specific behaviors. And if those behaviors are what you want to see repeated, it's important to encourage them and give feedback on that as well.

Getting your business in order, you may have noticed, is a matter of not only the logistics of how you do things, but also the human aspect of those you serve and the team who help you do it. Neither should ever be neglected. No matter how long you've been in business or how successful you become, distractions of any kind have the power to shift your attention. Ask Tory Johnson, the *New York Times* bestseller of *Shift for Good*, a regular on *Good Morning America,* and a long-time successful business leader I've followed and admired for years. She's spoken of a time when her businesses needed her, but her attention was redirected by certain experiences in her life, and she had checked out of her day-to-day responsibilities. As I was reading the rawness of what she shared, I was stopped in my tracks by what she said: "I violated a golden rule: Value the folks who row for you and keep them happy and engaged." Such a statement is important to remember when you are navigating the waters of being a small business CEO leader and building a business that's making an impact in the marketplace. Creating and keeping track of what is important and paying attention to what's in front of you makes the biggest difference in how you and your brand will succeed.

I've known Delmar in a professional capacity for five plus years. For the last two years we've contracted Delmar Johnson for her Human Resource brain (expertise!) to our group of over 350 entrepreneurs. Delmar is highly knowledgeable in the area of assisting entrepreneurs and organizations looking to grow and leverage human capital, build teams, and reduce the risk of potential issues within their organizational structure. Outside of our live teaching environment, we often refer Delmar to our network of over 12,000 members of entrepreneurs and small business owners. If you're looking to hire a speaker or trainer who can deliver strong, reliable, and relevant HR strategies, stop looking—and hire Delmar. She's consistent and simply knows her stuff!

Aprille Franks, CEO
Coach, Speak & Serve
www.aprillefranks.com

CHAPTER 10

Boost Your Company Efficiency

Streamline your HR department

Everyone is pressed for time these days. Your to-do lists turn into a *how will I get it all done* frenzy. The challenge is finding the best ways to save time while increasing efficiency in your HR functions. The more time- and labor-saving techniques you can identify and implement, the more opportunities are available to add to the bottom line. With all the moving parts and measures of accountability found inside a human resources department, there is no time to waste on inserting more standardized processes. Below are four ways to help you craft an efficiency blueprint that has the potential to positively impact your productivity:

1) Cut your paper load and go digital

Think back about twenty years ago; the idea of a paperless office was nerve-wracking to those of us who were just getting used to the idea of the up-and-coming technology hacks. Sure, we had access to the technology of the day, but it had its limitations. The tech super-gadgets of today that let us get things done quicker have us all spoiled. Although the concept of the paperless office rang around the globe, it lacked accuracy.

In human resources, documentation is like breathing; it's an everyday occurrence. It is significant for tracking information, feedback, and employee relations issues of all kinds. There's a saying I've adopted unofficially after being in HR all these years, and that is, *if it's not written down, it didn't happen.* I can't take credit for that mantra, but it's always had some validity to it in my opinion. The question to ask is, how do you manage all the paper that continues to flow through HR offices everywhere, even today? Instead of tracking down physical files, adopting a document management platform to simplify and streamline locating paperwork digitally has several benefits, like the following:

- Quicker access to employee files through an HR information database

- Digitally captures and stores documents in one central location

- Password accessible, maintaining the integrity of private information

- Takes up a lot less space in the office

- Easy to go back and edit information as necessary

- Personnel files and other documents become portable

That list is only the tip of the iceberg, but you get the idea. The paperless office may never truly become a reality; however, it can be fun trying.

2) Outsource what you can

Human resources is a big job with big responsibilities, and it takes a village to make things run like a well-oiled machine. You're responsible not only for being a strategic partner in carrying out the vision of the business, but also for all the moving parts, including recruiting, payroll, legal compliance, benefits, and more. That can feel a little overwhelming. One day you feel like you're the captain of the ship and the next you have a sinking experience.

Here are some numbers to consider. According to a 2014 survey by the SCORE Association, a nonprofit supported by the US Small Business Administration, the average small business owner spends up to 25 percent of his or her time handling employee-related paperwork. This average can increase to a staggering 35 to 45 percent if the tasks include recruitment, hiring, and training of new employees. HR outsourcing options save business owners time by taking on this burdensome responsibility while helping them remain compliant with the relevant laws.

3) Computerize the recruiting process

From my long-term experience in HR, I've learned that one of the key areas that typically takes the most time to complete is hiring staff. Statistically, it can take as many as three months or more to hire one person. That can be very frustrating, particularly to a small business owner—and as a side note, this is the very reason why I frequently tell clients that attracting and recruiting a good-fit employee usually takes patience and time. It doesn't stop them from getting frustrated, but the forewarning is important. Computerized recruiting is generally paperless and makes the process a lot less complicated and time-consuming, but it's not without flaws. Granted, the hiring process involves so much more; however, there are some steps that are no longer constrained to manual operations because of the digital age; for example, steps like manually sourcing resumes or logging applicants by way of spreadsheets, or having to do all of the recruitment process in-house. HR automation has changed the game.

4) Create processes for organization
As talked about in chapter 9, getting organized in the operations of your business will save you time, headaches, and money. Developing processes that others can follow when you are not there is the ultimate goal, so that you will be able to "fire" yourself from the daily grind of working *in* your business and instead be working *on* your business as the CEO that you are.

Start creating your own SOP. Below is a sample SOP layout, only one of many versions you can use.

HR Is Sexy!

LOGO 1

Page SOP Template [Your Title]

Created by: Version #, MM/DD/YY   Approved by: Date of approval:

SOP Name: Enter SOP Name

Purpose: Enter high level overview of the purpose

Scope: Enter high level description of the scope of the procedure

Definitions: Sample, an example showing the correct use SOP Standard Operating Procedure

Description: 1 Page SOP Template

Procedure:

Step #1: - Instructions
          Instructions

Step #2: - Instructions
          Instructions

Step #3: - Instructions
          Instructions

Tools and automation

Just as there are risks taken in business to grow and expand, none of that would be possible in the current marketplace without the necessary tools and automation capabilities of today's technology. When these are incorporated into your strategic business practices, the potential for success is exponentially increased. Whether you are just starting out or considered a more established business, technology will and does play a significant part in how you run your business daily. The list can be very long when it comes to today's technology options; below are just a few tools that have the capability to create more organization and efficiency in your business:

For customer relations management:
- Infusionsoft
- Ontraport
- Kartra

Human resources automation databases:
- Paychex
- ADP
- Gusto

For team and project management:
- Teamwork
- Trello
- Basecamp

Digital courses and training portals:
- Kajabi
- Teachable
- Thinkific

Final Thoughts

It almost goes without saying that the relationship between being an entrepreneur and growing a business, and how human resources plays a strategic part, is all an intricate dance. With all the moving pieces of establishing and growing a successful business, one of the biggest pieces is people. Beyond the people are laws, systems, policies, and so much more that establish effective best practices to serve those people. As much as entrepreneurs may prefer to focus on the more glamorous side of things, like clients, making money, and selling their products and services, none of it is sustainable without an infrastructure to build upon. That is why *HR Is Sexy!*

HR Is Sexy is more than just a concept, it's also a reference tool. The vision is to positively impact the global entrepreneur community. It represents an opportunity to connect you to others who are likeminded and who completely get the highs and lows of growing a business that will thrive in the marketplace.

I encourage you to connect with us on Facebook and Instagram and join hundreds of others who are tapping into the HR Is Sexy experience. For additional resources and to connect with other HR Is Sexy enthusiasts, visit www.thehresuite.com and join the community.

Thank you for buying and reading this book. If you adopt these concepts and implement them in your business, I believe you will come to see this as one of your best investments of your time and money. If *HR Is Sexy* makes a difference for you, share it with your fellow entrepreneurs and influencers. I would love to hear how you've applied the points presented throughout the book to your business for greater effectiveness and efficiency.

Wishing you continued success!

Delmar

Connect with Delmar

You can find me online on your favorite social media platforms at the following links:

https://www.facebook.com/delmar.johnson1
https://linkedin.com/in/delmarjohnson1/
https://www.instagram.com/smallbizhrcoach/
https://twitter.com/HRBrainforHire
https://www.delmarjohnson.com/
https://hrbrainforhire.com/

About the Author

Delmar Johnson is an HR specialist and consultant, as well as the founder and CEO of Delmar Johnson Enterprises, LLC. She has a master's degree in organizational management/human resources, and through her business HR Brain for Hire™, she helps first-time employers and growing businesses who are in need of assistance with human resources and don't know where to start. Delmar is passionate about empowering women who are in the middle of career transitions by helping them think differently about what they're able to do and has made it her personal mission to use her gifts of encouragement, intelligence, and resilience to make an impact through inspiring and cultivating the self-worth and power of women. In 2018, Delmar received the Spark and Hustle Small Business Resiliency Award. Delmar lives in Memphis, and in her free time she enjoys watching movies, traveling, bowling, listening to podcasts, and reading.

To learn more, visit www.delmarjohnson.com

HR e-SUITE FOR ENTREPRENEURS
AND PROFESSIONALS

The HR eSuite is so much more than an HR Help Desk; it is a platform for community, education, and growth. The HR eSuite will guide and coach you through HR best practices that position you to scale and sustain your business through team building, training, and development and compliance measures.

Find more information at www.thehresuite.com

Join Now @ www.thehresuite.com

www.ingramcontent.com/pod-product-compliance
Lightning Source LLC
Chambersburg PA
CBHW071642210326
41597CB00017B/2084